The Honest Truth about
Donald Trump

ROBBY CAMPBELL

Copyright © 2018 Robby Campbell
All rights reserved
First Edition

PAGE PUBLISHING, INC.
New York, NY

First originally published by Page Publishing, Inc. 2018

ISBN 978-1-64350-382-0 (Paperback)
ISBN 978-1-64350-383-7 (Digital)

Printed in the United States of America

This book is dedicated to my loving wife, Helen, who did so much work to make this book possible.

Robby Campbell

Contents

Preface 7
Introduction 9

The Honest Truth about Donald Trump 11
About Donald John Trump and Family 15
Items President Trump Must Deal With 25
Trump the Candidate 30
Republican Candidates 37
President Trump's Political Strategy 38
President Trump's Income Tax Return 41
Russia 42
Trump and People of Other Ethnicities 45
Liberal Democrats 46
Obama's Shadow Government 48
Organizing for Action 49
Radicalism 50
Voter Fraud 51
Education 52
Election Laws 53
Judicial Restraint 54
Foreign Relations 55
ISIS and Terrorists 58
Protesters/Demonstrators 59
Fake/Fraud News 60
Political Appointees 64
Health Care: "Obamacare" 65
Veterans/Military/First Responders 67
Barack Obama: Personal 70

Barack Obama: The Politician 73
Barack Obama and Communism 76
Race Relations 78
The Muslim Culture 79
Disloyal Holdovers 84
Abortion/Pro-Life 85
Gun Control 86
Economy/Jobs 87
Immigration 90
The Story about Old White Men 99

Conclusion 101
Survey of World War II Veterans (44) 103
Funny Questions 108

Preface

My reason for writing this book is that I am disappointed to the point of being outraged about the way President Donald Trump is being treated by the liberal fraud media, liberal Democrats, and establishment Republicans. I am also outraged by the other hate groups and organizations that vehemently say and write terrible things about him. Most of these ugly attacks are lies and spin stories to belittle President Trump and to halt his agenda.

Former President Obama's shadow presidency and the Organizing for Action group that numbers in the thousands are doing all they can to undermine President Trump. Obama is in control of all these shadow government organizations of agitators and activists whose sole purpose is to destroy Mr. Trump's success as president.

The other main purpose of Organizing for Action is to preserve Obama's legacy. Only time will tell us who will win this battle for who the leaders of this country will be. I believe it will be President Trump who wins this battle for leadership and to take this country in the right direction to "make America great again." We can hope and pray that President Trump's America first agenda will continue into the future years of this great country.

Some of the information and quotes in this book are from e-mails received from friends. These e-mails did not indicate an author's name or source of the information.

My intent is not to attack or slander the people I disagree with but to attack the people who go to rallies, television shows, and radio talk shows and rant and slander conservatives, Republicans, and President Trump. I respect and give credit to their private personal lives. They may be good citizens, have a great family, teach Sunday school, and go to church. This is good, and I congratulate them for their success and accomplishments in their private lives.

In this book, I mention several times that President Trump thinks, talks, and acts like a person of the World War II generation. One example of this is how he is much like President Harry Truman. A news media person wrote a story about President Truman, and in the story, he mentioned that President Truman's daughter, Margaret, played the piano very poorly. President Truman believed in supporting his family. He gave the news media person a tongue-lashing, which appeared in all the newspapers for several days, and he mentioned it a few times in his speeches thereafter. President Truman believed in making the tough decisions (drop the atomic bombs on Japan) even if it was hard to do and unpopular. President Truman fired General Douglas McArthur, the supreme commander of the Korean War. President Trump supports his family and fires people when it is the right thing to do. He is also good at making hard decisions that must be made.

Introduction

One of my reasons for writing this book is that I am a very strong supporter of President Donald Trump and his agenda. I hope this book defines how I believe President Trump will be a very great and successful president for our country.

My other reason for writing this book is that my pastor, Dr. Robert Jeffress, is a big supporter of President Trump. I have heard all the positive things he has said in meetings, on Fox TV news programs, and in many interviews on talk radio. What I have heard him say is very good and positive about his personal friend, President Trump. I respect and admire all the great, positive information Dr. Jeffress has said about President Trump. For these and many other good reasons, I believe President Trump is the right person at this time to be president of the United States of America.

We have been very fortunate at First Baptist Church of Dallas because we have had great pastors over many years. Dr. George W. Truett was the pastor for forty years. He built First Baptist Dallas into one of the first mega churches. President Woodrow Wilson asked him to serve as a military chaplain in World War I. There is a very interesting story about him on my blog (www.robby-campbell.blogpot.com). Dr. Truett is world-famous as a great pastor, author, and leader of the World War II generation.

Dr. W. A. Criswell was pastor of First Baptist Dallas for over fifty years. He is world-famous as a pastor and author of many books that Christian seminaries use to teach their students how to be successful pastors. Dr. Criswell had much influence in many of the good things that happened in the Christian community of Dallas from the early 1940s to the 1990s.

Dr. Robert Jeffress is from the same mold as Dr. Truett and Dr. Criswell. He is world-renowned today because of his personal relationship with President Trump. Dr. Jeffress preached a sermon to the president, Vice President Pence, and their families a few hours before he was sworn in as president of the United States. His ministry is worldwide on television, radio, and Internet. Dr. Jeffress's Christian ministry is reaching more of the world with additional radio and television broadcasts.

The Honest Truth about Donald Trump

This book is about President Donald Trump. First, I want to establish my credibility. I was born in 1926 in Mount Vernon, Franklin County, Texas. My birth certificate and discharge papers were in the county clerk's office. I served in WWII in the US Navy. I was in Okinawa when the war ended. My three brothers also served in WWII. Two were in the army, and one was in the air force. I hold a bachelor of science degree from the University of Houston and a master of education degree from Texas A&M University in Commerce, Texas (formerly East Texas State College). Enough said about me. If you want to know more about me, I am on your computer in three different ways:

1. My blog www.robby-campbell.blogspot.com. This blog has stories mostly about people I know who served in WWII.
2. www.generationsbroadcastcenter.com. You may choose to watch the introductory video. My story may be seen by clicking on Oral Histories, then Veterans Oral Histories, then WWII. Pictures are listed in alphabetical order by last name. Click on "Campbell" or another last name to see individual interviews. This website has about 120 personal stories (about twenty minutes each) of men and women who are from the WWII generation.
3. Orville Rogers and I were interviewed on www.youtube.com. Click on Kandi Rose (enter). Click on her picture to see her addiction-free ministry. Kandi was visiting with Susie Jennings, founder of Operation Care International,

at the Christmas party for homeless and poor people at the Dallas Convention Center when the interview took place.

    I do not know President Trump personally. I've never been in a room with him or been to any of his political rallies. However, I have had a friend for fifty years who does know him personally. He was very active in his presidential campaign. My information about President Trump is what I have heard my friend say many times about his close relationship with Mr. Trump. He flew with Mr. Trump on his private airplane to campaign with him in different states. When he goes to New York, which he does frequently, he visits with Mr. Trump in the Trump Tower and visits with the Trump family. My information is from this friend. My friend believes that Mr. Trump has wisdom and intelligence far better than most people. He talks about his sense of humor and humility. He loves the United States and wants to make this a better country in so many ways. My friend states that Mr. Trump is a devout Christian who loves and respects people of all races and religions.
    He believes in the Constitution of the United States, and the people in government work for the people, not the other way around. He believes that state government has a lot of control over what happens in this country by working with the federal government. The friend who has said many great and positive things about President Trump is mentioned on the Introduction page.
    President Trump urges our national leadership to protect and defend our natural and constitutional rights and swiftly wage successful war on terrorists. President Trump always states his concerns in direct agreement with the US Constitution. His dealmaking ability will always be to encourage the House, Senate, and Supreme Court to always consider the Constitution when dealing with US law.
    President Trump urges Congress to adopt a Constitutional Restoration Act and support the principle of judicial restraint, which requires judges to interpret and apply rather than make the law. He supports judges who strictly interpret the law based on its original intent. He opposes judges who assume for themselves legislative powers. He calls on Congress and the president to use their consti-

tutional powers to restrain activist judges. What President Trump is promoting is an interesting story about old white men. Old white men in the last few years have endured with tolerance a lot of criticism by liberals.

My reason for writing this book is that I feel like millions of viewers of cable TV and talk radio people listening to liberal media, which make up 90 percent of the news media and are liberal. I think those millions are very much like me—listening to this stuff makes your brain almost explode, and you have a heavy heart because of what the liberals are saying and doing to this great country. Anyone listening to all the different news media is confused and frustrated, just as I am. Here's why: Who can you believe when you are watching TV or listening to radio? They are talking about a specific news story on TV or radio and giving their point of view. Then you change your TV channel or radio station, and they are giving the same story with a completely different opinion. The opinions are 100 percent opposite. Who do you believe?

We all know Donald Trump is not the normal run-of-the-mill politician. He does not act or talk like most politicians. His way of getting a job or project completed successfully is in a unique business way. He has intelligence and personality working for him. He closes most deals to make sure the deal is in his favor. It doesn't matter if it is a business project or a political project; you must have the skill to close the deal in your favor to be successful. For many years, President Trump has been very successful in building a business. Now in his first one hundred days as president, he has placed this country on the right track to "make America great again."

Many people are sick and tired of most politicians who mealy-mouth about where they stand when they are asked political questions or they give a long-winded spin answer that leaves you wondering what they said and where they stand on your question. President Trump answers questions like normal everyday people, not like most politicians. Because of who and what he is, the president gives us great hope and good feelings about the things he will do for this country in the future. I believe he talks and acts like people of the World War II generation.

From this point on, I will be telling you what I believe about President Trump and how I came to believe it. I am retired and have a lot of free time. I am politically active and go to a lot of political meetings, and I belong to a political PAC that does a lot of research on people in politics. I watch four to six hours of cable TV news every day. I listen to talk radio during the day and read many articles in magazines that are politically oriented. I'm very fortunate to have friends who are very active in politics and have a lot of inside information about local, state, and federal politicians. So from all these people who have given me a great deal of information about politics, I think I have a good background to say what I will about President Trump.

About Donald John Trump and Family

To really know Donald Trump, you must know his family. The Trump family story is a very American story. Donald Trump's grandparents immigrated to the United States from Kallstadt, Germany, which, throughout history, has been alternately French and German; the Trumps are German. Fred Trump, Donald's father, died in 1999 at age ninety-four. He was beloved and worth between $250 and $300 million. His wife died a year later.

Donald John Trump was born on June 16, 1946. He was seventy years old on Election Day. He was born fourth of five children over an eleven-year period. He was born and raised in Queens, New York. The family lived in the estates section of Queens. The Trump home was a larger version of the homes his father, Fred, built for his tenants. Fred was a very successful home builder who built homes for World War II veterans. Donald was never a "preppy," and he never embraced any aspect of the "hippie" movement. His secondary schooling was at New York Military Academy. He was generally popular in high school and made friends easily. Donald attended Fordham University in New York City for two years and transferred to the University of Pennsylvania Wharton School of Business. At that time, the Wharton School offered a rare program for real estate business. This is where Donald became interested in the real estate business. We all know how well he has done in real estate.

His older brother, Fred Jr., died in early adulthood because of complications from alcoholism. The experience of losing his older brother to alcoholism had a lasting effect on Donald. He does not smoke, drink alcohol, or use recreational drugs. Of the last four presidents, he is the only one who has not smoked weed. His doctor publicly announced Mr. Trump to be in excellent health. He was a very good high school athlete in football, soccer, and especially baseball.

He had potential to become a professional. Mr. Trump has been married three times. His first wife, Ivana, was an immigrant from Czechoslovakia and a divorcee, who has been married four times in her life. She is a lifelong avid skier and worked in design at the Trump organization. Marla Maples, Trump's second wife, is an actress and model. His third wife, Melania, is an immigrant from Slovenia (born in Yugoslavia) and has been a supermodel. Trump's oldest daughter, Ivanka, and her three children are Jewish. Ivanka converted to Judaism upon marrying Jared Kushner. He is a very successful businessman and is now on President Trump's staff.

President Trump has the right attitude about marriage and family. Although he has been married three times, he respects and loves all of them and the children they had together. He supports the definition of marriage as a God-ordained, legal and moral commitment only between a natural man and a natural woman. He opposes the assault on marriage by judicial activists. Homosexuality must not be presented as an acceptable alternative lifestyle in public policy, nor should family be redefined to include homosexual couples. A good story that goes along with attitude about marriage—let boys marry boys and let girls marry girls, and in one generation, there won't be any Democrats!

Donald Trump did not serve in Vietnam. He was not drafted due to bone spurs in his heels. Ultimately, he was in the draft lottery and drew a high number.

Mr. Trump started his business career in an office he shared with his father in Sheepshead Bay, Brooklyn, New York. He worked with his father for five years where they were busy making deals together. Donald has been quoted as saying "my father was my mentor, and I learned a tremendous amount about every aspect of the construction industry from him." Likewise, Fred C. Trump often stated, "Some of my best deals were made by my son, Donald—everything he touches seems to turn to gold." After spending those five years working with his father, Donald entered the very different world of Manhattan real estate. This took courage to start doing business in Manhattan, New York, one of the toughest cities in which to be successful. Donald was successful, not because he is a penny-pincher, but because he is thrifty with money.

Mr. Trump was the original owner of the New Jersey Generals of the US Football League. He sold the franchise so he would be free for construction projects. This information about Donald's early years shows us how he analyzes the project at hand and does what is necessary to make the project a success. This should give people of this country great comfort to see how he will perform as president of the United States.

Mr. Trump's Christian church is Presbyterian, and the Holy Bible is his favorite book. People who know him personally say he is a born-again Christian believer and that this is a nation under God founded by Judeo-Christian principles. He affirms the constitutional right of all individuals to worship as they choose.

> We affirm that the public acknowledgment of God is undeniable in our history and is vital to our freedom, prosperity and strength. We pledge our influence toward a return to the original intent of the first amendment and toward dispelling the myth of a separation of church and state.

Donald Trump can truthfully say he has a family that everyone can be proud of. How he treats his wife and children in public shows his love for them and sets a good example for all men. Donald Trump has a philosophy that supports the definition of family and marriage as a God-ordained, legal, and moral commitment only between a natural man and a natural woman. He believes that parental rights, authority, and responsibility are inherent and protected by the US Constitution. "Local, state, or federal laws, regulations, or policies shall not be enacted that limit rights in the rearing of both biological and adopted children." Parents have the right and responsibility to direct and guide their children's moral education.

Donald Trump is the greatest career adviser of the baby boomer generation. Donald has reached the zenith in his careers as book author, TV entertainer, sports entertainer, real estate developer, and currently politician. He has authored more than eighteen books. At least one of them, *The Art of the Deal*, was a top seller. President Trump does not accept a salary for being president of the United States; each month, he gives the check to a different charity. Mr. Trump likes golf, and he has developed eleven golf courses, which bear his name. He has been nominated twice for an Emmy Award. He has a star on the Hollywood Walk of Fame. He has been inducted into the Professional Wrestling Hall of Fame. He has appeared in more than a dozen movies such as *Home Alone 2*, *Zoolander*, and *Little Rascals*. Trump has been the executive producer of seven television shows. He has been the guest host of five television shows such as *Extra*, *Larry King Live*, *Saturday Night Live*, and more. He has been a coproducer of the longest-running reality show. Trump performed in several WWE wrestling shows. He performed in WrestleMania 23, which set attendance records and revenue records up until that time.

Keeping in mind that 90 percent of start-up businesses fail, Trump's record of enterprise is nothing short of amazing. He has enjoyed success in at least eleven very different enterprises—professional football, ice-skating rinks, fragrance, ice, steaks, wines, model management, airline blenders, menswear, bicycle races, world-class beauty contests, and many others. In some of these, such as model management, his firm has risen to the top of that industry. Trump Entertainment, casinos and resorts, was recently sold to Carl Icahn. His personal managing of the Wollman Ice-Skating Rink in the early 1980s is the quintessential case study for MBA students in Wharton, Harvard University, and other business schools. Donald's performance there was phenomenal. His privately held businesses have employed more than two hundred thousand people. In the casino business in Atlantic City, Trump had to do business with known mobsters, and he stayed "clean" and alive. Aside from his personal investments, he has never been a Wall Street "player."

Donald J. Trump is the very definition of the American success story, continually setting the standards of excellence in business, real estate, and entertainment. In New York City and around the world, the Trump signature is synonymous with the most prestigious of addresses. Among them are the world-renowned Fifth Avenue skyscraper, Trump Tower, and the luxurious residential buildings: Trump Park, Trump Palace, Trump Plaza, 610 Park Avenue, Trump World Tower (the tallest building on the east side of Manhattan), and Trump Park Avenue. President Trump was also responsible for the designation and construction of the Jacob Javits Convention Center on land controlled by him, known as the West 34 Street Railroad Yards, and the total exterior restoration of the Grand Central Station terminal as part of his conversion of the neighboring Commodore Hotel into the Grand Hyatt Hotel. This development is considered one of the most successful restorations in the city and earned Donald Trump an award from Manhattan Community Board Five for the "tasteful and creative recycling of a distinguished hotel."

Information about the political Trump:

- 1967–1987   Democrat
- 1987–1999   Republican
- 1999–2001   Reform Party (Ross Perot)
- 2001–2009   Democrat
- 2009–2011   Republican
- 2011–2012   Independent
- 2012–present   Republican

Mr. Trump has an extraordinarily energetic central nervous system, much like Teddy Roosevelt but more targeted to industry and enterprise. Donald Trump's presidency will be very energetic, transparent, and communicative. He will be a very hardworking president. His interaction with his older brother (whom everybody loved) tells that he thinks everyone is like him or wants to be or should be. His relationship with his older brother was a hard lesson in tolerance for him. Trump's son, Donald Jr., is right when he said his dad is a "blue-collar billionaire." Donald Trump's children are very important to him and it shows. All his family and friends are very important to him. When you study and observe Donald Trump, you see a person who is a good listener to other people. He makes a special effort to show respect for everyone; that is, unless they attack him or show disrespect toward him. That is when Trump does not let attacks and disrespect go unchallenged. He attacks back and most times is stronger than the attacker, and he doubles down many times to make sure the attacker knows how he feels.

Most people agree with the way Trump attacks and fights back at the fraud liberal news media. The fraud liberal news media deserves what he gives then because they are so corrupt and dishonest with how they treat Republicans and conservative people. Donald Trump treats most people with straight talk and respect. Trump has a personality with a warm charm and love for people. He also has a great sense of humor and loves to cut up and interact with people. Trump shows his love for his family and children in public and, I'm sure, at home in private ways. Donald has helped his grown children to be very mature, nice citizens. They are likeable and have a friendly personality that anyone enjoys being their friend. His grown children all have a good education, and they all have been successful in the business world of their choice.

Trump tweets mostly about government and politics, but some of the most interesting tweets are about family and children, for example, how they enjoy family get-togethers and having a big family meal together. He says one of the most rewarding things in his life is when he does outings in love and fellowship with his family. This kind of attitude is what millions of people noticed about Trump and got him elected president of the United States. Of course, this is not the only reason he was elected president. Trump's work ethic, of working sixteen to eighteen hours a day and being able to get by on four or five hours of sleep each night shows how hard he works. Many people who have worked with him over the years on large and small projects say how well he listens and takes advice and learns from others.

I have mentioned several times in this book that President Trump thinks, talks, and acts like the people of the World War II generation. Now I want to have a strong discussion to go into detail about what I meant by this statement. In my opinion, the people of the World War II generation had common sense, honesty, and personal responsibility that caused that generation to be the strong conservatives that believed in supporting unity of country over political party. This attitude does great things for your country and wins wars. When this country faces a crisis, you consider what is best for America. Then all government officials, politicians, and citizens unite to do what is best for the country. President Trump in his speeches and executive order legislation passed are great for this country. His agenda to be passed in the future are health care, tax reform, southern border wall, job-training poor people, improving and cleaning up poor communities, and bringing manufacturing companies and jobs back to America. This is just a start of all the good things he has on his agenda. Mr. Trump will do whatever it takes to make this country great again and make the people successful. He considers what is the right thing to do, not just what is popular with people.

Like the World War II generation and President Trump, just be plain and simple and do the right thing. To me, President Trump talks in a way that is not political. That is why he is president—he talks common sense, not the Washington, DC.

Spin and mealymouth beat-around-the-bush talk you hear from so many Washington, DC, politicians. Like my generation, we talk to people in very down-to-earth and straightforward language that all can appreciate and understand. When President Trump is verbally attacked, he attacks back, and this is good. This is the mind-set of the World War II generation and President Trump—don't let people lie and slander you. Fight back and make sure you win with an aggressive counterattack. We believe you must always be willing to stand up and defend yourself and your country. When you live in the greatest country the world has ever known, you do what you must to be loyal to yourself and your country. I think that most people who love this country feel that way. President Trump has expressed many times how the past administration did such a poor job of telling the world how wonderful and great the United States of America is.

The World War II generation could handle the truth. President Roosevelt and his administration kept the people informed. They told us the good and the bad of what was happening in World War II. The newspapers were not censored, nor were the movie picture news reels. President Trump is very open and trustworthy with what he tells the people about what is happening in his administration. I hope he will keep tweeting because this is his way of going directly to the people with his message.

I believe most of the people want President Trump to keep tweeting. We appreciate that he is talking directly to us. The present-day generation can also handle the truth. By tweeting, he bypasses the fake media people who would take what he says and spin it in a dishonest way to make President Trump look bad, even if it is a good report of the news. The fake news media, television, radio, and newspapers are against most of President Trump's agenda. I think they lie and spin what President Trump says, even when they know what he is saying is good for the country. They are so dishonest in the way they report his information that they border on being disloyal to the United States. Thank goodness, we did not have fake news people in the World War II days.

My three brothers and I served in World War II. Two of my brothers served in Europe in the army. My older brother, Buddy, had an outstanding war record. He went into Normandy on D-day. He served in northern France, Rhineland, Ardennes, and Central Europe. He received the Good Conduct Medal, American Defense Service Medal, Legion of Merit Medal, Campaign Medal with five bronze stars, and the Purple Heart. He was wounded while building a pontoon bridge across the Rhine River. I served in the navy in the Pacific and was in Okinawa when the war ended. We had great support and loyalty from President Roosevelt and President Truman. They always had our back. President Trump is like Roosevelt and Truman. The active military of today is comfortable and at ease with President Trump. He is loyal and absolutely supports the troops. He is doing everything that he can to build the military services back to being the best and strongest military power in the world. His military budget will give better training and better equipment to all branches of the military units. President Trump has made it very clear how much he appreciates what the military does for our country.

President Trump has made it very clear how he feels about veterans. He has passed legislation that will give veterans' hospitals more money to give veterans quicker access to doctors for treatment of their needs. If a veteran cannot quickly get into a veterans' hospital, they are given government document that will allow treatment in a close public hospital. President Trump also appointed outstanding administrators to be in charge of improving all the duties and responsibilities for better care of veterans. If you watch President Trump at rallies and meetings of all kinds, he always recognizes and honors with great respect the veterans and active military. All the veterans and active military that I know support, honor, and respect President Trump for the way he treats them. In the 2016 election, the large majority of the active military and the veterans voted for Trump over Clinton. All the good things that I said about how President Trump supports the veterans and active military, you truly could say he has honored and supported the policies that serve and enforce the laws of this country. President Trump never seems to be at a loss for words when he gives praise and thanks in public for what they do to keep law and order in this country. Just consider what it would be like to live in a country without the military and police. In the 2016 election, the police showed how they felt about Donald Trump because the majority of police officers voted for Mr. Trump.

I could stop talking about veterans, active military, and the police, but before I do, I believe President Trump has a heartfelt concern for what these organizations do for the people of our country. Put yourself in their place. You are a soldier on patrol in Syria to stop 1515 terrorist soldiers from killing men, women, and children. Those 1515 soldiers will kill or capture you and torch you to death. How would you feel if this were to happen to you? Put yourself in the place of a police officer giving a traffic ticket to a reckless driver. The driver pulls a gun and shoots you six times; how do you feel? This is the reason President Trump is so supportive of the military and police. Whenever he can, he gives a good report about the veterans, military, and police in his speeches.

I have mentioned my blog several times. Now I want to give you specific details of what this blog is about. It is mostly about the great men and women who lived their lives in the years of the World War II generation—the 1920s to the 1960s; I have said that President Trump thinks, talks, and acts like this generation. To understand what I am saying, I need to give you information and stories about people of the World War II period. My blog starts with stories about the Civil War, World War I, mostly World War II, Korean War, and Vietnam War and stories about Iraq and Afghanistan. There are also some interesting special stories. My blog also gives information on how to see 120 personal, twenty-minute interviews given by people of that era. When you read and listen to these stories, you will have a greater understanding of how the World War II generation thinks, talks, and acts. I also believe you will see that people of the World War II generation and President Trump have very much in common.

Items President Trump Must Deal With

Vladimir Putin: He is a very clever, complex leader with a KGB background that gives him a ruthless mind-set. That means he is not easy to understand or to deal with. He has the reputation of double-talk when dealing with other nations; that means he will not always keep his word. To say it another way, he will say or do whatever it takes to make sure he gets what is best for Russia. Regarding the collusion story about how Russia was involved in our 2016 presidential election, Putin does a great job of making this story work to his advantage. Putin has used the collusion story to cause all kinds of problems with Democrats and Republicans to spend so much time dealing with it.

Russian Troops in Syria: Why are they there and what are they doing? No nation has an answer to this question. This is just a small part of the problems Russia is causing President Trump to deal with. With his skills and ability to make deals, he is doing much better than the previous administration. President Trump has a much better communication and friendly relationship with Putin than Obama had. For these reasons, President Trump will have a better working relationship than the Obama administration.

Immigration: This is a problem that everyone has an opinion about. Most Americans agree on legal immigration, and most Americans disagree with illegal immigrants entering our country. Most Americans agree we should build the southern border wall and stop illegals and drugs from crossing the southern border. President

Trump agrees with this last statement because he always agrees with "America first." His executive order that puts tighter restrictions on illegal immigrants entering this country has been very effective. Seventy percent fewer people are crossing our borders now. The Supreme Court's new travel law about who can enter this country is a good law. President Trump's attitude is this is what we must do to keep the country safe for all our people.

Trump Health Care: This is still a work in progress that must be continued until we have a new health-care plan. Obama's affordable health-care plan is a disaster and must be replaced with a health-care plan that gives better hospital card and costs less. President Trump realizes that health care is one-sixth of the US economy. He is personally involved in working with the House and Senate leadership to be successful in getting a new and better health-care plan. I believe President Trump will be successful in getting a new health-care plan because of his leadership and deal-making skills.

Tax Reform: This legislation must happen soon if the US economy improves and grows stronger. President Trump has tax reform at the top of his list of what must be accomplished. He realizes that to accomplish all his agenda plans, it will take more money going to the Department of Treasury. With tax reform and new money coming in, he will be able to do all the great things, short term and long term, that will make this "country great again."

Leaks: This is a big problem that must be stopped. President Trump understands that the first step is to remove all the disloyal Obama holdovers from his administration. He knows for a fact that they are the people who have caused most of the leak problems. The president strongly believes that all the people who work for him must be loyal to him. As a successful businessman, he built a business empire on experienced, qualified, loyal people. This is the same formula he is now using to build a group of loyal people around him to stop the leaks that cause serious problems in business as well as in government. President Trump will demand complete loyalty or disloyal people will be fired. In his first few months in office, he has already shown what he will do if you are disloyal—you're fired! President Trump knows that firing people is not an easy or pleasant thing to do. This is the example of what he has always done—do what is right, not what is easy.

Tweeting: This is a very big deal with a lot of people. The president can go directly to millions of people with his message. This is important because the fake news media cannot take what he says and spin it in a dishonest way to make what said into what they want the public to think he said. In my opinion, he should keep tweeting—we want to hear your message directly from you. I believe most fair and balanced people think when you are attacked, you have the right to attack back. The fake news media are the ones who first started attacking President Trump in a very vicious and dishonest way. In other places of this book, I said President Trump thinks, talks, and acts like the World War II generation. This is the generation I grew up in. When I was a child, teenager, and adult, when someone called me a liar or slandered me, they had better be ready to defend themselves because I would attack them. This is the generation that fought World War II. We did believe in retreat or defense; we believed in offense (attacking). In business and as president of the United States, Mr. Trump has won by going on the offensive—attack! Have a backbone! That's the way to go!

Fake News: This is a problem that no other president has had to deal with. All our past presidents have had to deal with criticism from newspapers, television, and radio, but it was never as vicious and dishonest as it is today. Some of the cable news stations have gotten to the point that many people do not watch them because they are so negative and dishonest, and when you go to bed, you have a hard time going to sleep. Then when you finally go to sleep, you have bad dreams. Fake news is a very difficult problem to deal with. If you ignore it, people say you do not have a backbone. If you answer and fight back, people say you are mean and have thin skin. President Trump does what I think is the right way. Be a fighter, stand up for yourself, and attack back. President Trump has the right to defend himself and his family.

South Border Wall: President Trump and most Americans want America to be safe from illegal immigrants and free of drugs from Mexico. We want this wall to be built as soon as possible. One of the great new ideas is design polar panels on the wall to create energy and save money. I repeat, we all want legal immigration, not illegal immigration. One of the most important things about building a wall is that it will stop a lot of violence (shootings and deaths) between the border patrol and illegal immigrants. Landowners along the southern border have to put up with the killing of their cattle, theft of property, destroying cattle fences, polluting the water, and trash left on their land. This is just a few of the things that happen along the southern border. These incidents cause people living along the southern border to be armed with assault weapons or pay a lot of money for bodyguards. No one is pleased with the hardships and suffering that the illegals ensure, so what's the answer? President Trump says to have a better work permit system for temporary workers coming to our country. Also, treat these workers with dignity, respect, good pay, and good living conditions. President Trump is giving the right solutions for a better relationship with Mexico.

Terrorists: President Trump has a very clear straightforward way of dealing with all terrorists, that is, ISIS, Syria, Iran, Iraq, Afghanistan, and all the other terrorists. You do not negotiate with violent terrorists; you defeat and destroy them. This is quite different from the previous administration, which was not successful. Terrorism grew and expanded all over the world because Obama did very little to stop terrorism. President Trump has made it clear that he will attack and fight terrorism anywhere it exists. For example, when Assad used poison gas to kill men, women, and children, President Trump ordered a bombing air raid on Assad's air bases. If you remember, Obama drew a redline in Syria, threatening Assad if he used poison gas, which he did, and Obama did nothing. Assad used poison gas again. After President Trump bombed his air bases,

Assad has not used poison gas again. This is the way you must attack terrorism. Dictators and terrorists only respect strength with force to back it up. President Trump has made it clear in many ways that he will use the United States' strength with force to stop all terrorists.

Divided Country: This one of the most disappointing things that is happening in our country. President Trump, like most people, realizes that our country is divided—half conservative and half liberal, with a large group of independents that couldn't care less and are neither liberal nor conservative. They ignore all politics completely. President Trump is trying to get the two parties to work together, without much success. What needs to happen is that all politicians need to do what is best for the United States, not just what their political party is for or against. President Trump's agenda is what will make this country great again. What is stopping this from happening is the Democratic Party is obstructing at every turn. They do not want President Trump to be successful with any of his projects. Obstructive democrats oppose and vote against legislation even if it is the right project and good for the country. President Trump is doing the only thing he can in this situation. The majority of Republican Party should be loyal and stand 100 percent together and vote for what is good for the country. American voters need to be more informed about the politics of this country; take more interest in all elections, local and national; and know the political views of candidates for office. This is common sense—to set aside the time to really check out and be knowledgeable and informed about political candidates. When you do this, you elect qualified people for political offices. Then and only then will we have good diplomats in all political offices.

Some of President Trump's tweets are designed to bring this divided country together to do what is best for our country. Hopefully, with the president's deal-making and leadership ability, he will over time bring this divided country together and start thinking more about what is good for the United States and not what is good for their political party. The World War II generation was a success; President Trump will be a success.

Trump the Candidate

My first thought is, Why did Mr. Trump decide to run for president? I think he loves this country as much as anyone could love this country. He believed this country was in a very deep mess, and he thought he could change it for the better. With his background, he made the decision of what kind of political campaign he would run. We all know how this campaign would go. He realized his campaign had to be very different if he was to win the job.

Here are nine facts about President Trump's life that will give you a better understanding of who he is as a normal, commonsense person:

1. He almost filed for bankruptcy in 1990 due to massive personal and business debts. A significant amount of debt was garnered from financing the Taj Mahal, one of Trump's casinos acquired in 1988 through high-interest junk bonds. However, he ceded 50 percent ownership of the casino to the original bond holders who lowered Trump's interest rate and extended the loan so Trump had more time to pay off the debt. Today, Trump owns more than one hundred companies, and his net worth is approximately $4 billion.
2. The Trump World Tower, a residential skyscraper in Manhattan, has seventy-two completed floors (but lists ninety stories in the elevator panel). Before the Twenty-First-Century Tower in Dubai and Tower Place 3 in Seoul were built, the Trump World Tower was the largest residential building in the world.
3. President Trump has never done drugs, drank alcohol, or smoked cigarettes, and he is proud of it. His brother, Fred,

THE HONEST TRUTH ABOUT DONALD TRUMP

was an alcoholic and fought with addiction for many years, eventually dying from it. He warned young Donald never to go the same way, which he accepted to the letter.
4. Trump hosted his own reality TV show *The Apprentice* starting in 2004 on NBC. The purpose of the show was to eliminate contestants to find a head for one of Trump's companies. Trump was paid $375,000 per episode.
5. Trump's parents sent him to the New York Military Academy when he was age thirteen because he was an energetic child. They thought the institution would teach him some discipline. He graduated from the military academy in 1964 before continuing his education at Fordham University and eventually the University of Pennsylvania.
6. In 2007, Trump received his own Hollywood Walk of Fame star for his role as producer of *The Apprentice*. His star was the 2,327th added to the Walk of Fame.
7. Trump has had three wives—Ivana (1977–1992), Marla Maples (1993–1997), and Melania Knauss (2005 to present). Altogether, Trump has five children, including Donald Jr. (1977), Ivanka (1981), Eric (1984), Tiffany (1993), and Barron (2006).
8. Trump is the only presidential candidate with his own board game, Trump Game. The game was released in 1988 and requires players to invest in real estate properties while simultaneously attempt to bankrupt competitors.
9. Trump has owned the Miss Universe Organization since 1996. In 2003, NBC became a joint partner of the organization with Trump. The Miss Universe Organization also produces the Miss USA and Miss Teen USA Pageants.

When you read this information about President Trump, you realize what a diverse and knowledgeable person he is. He has been involved in a wide range of businesses in his fifty years in the business world. This background is just another reason why President Trump is experienced and qualified to be our president.

I could go on and on, but we all are witnesses to Mr. Trump's campaign. The things President Trump did in his campaign and is doing now as president are thought out and talked about before he says them. Why do I think this? Because most of the things he says and does now worked in his campaign and they work for him now as president of the United States of America.

President Trump is a brilliant genius because of what he has accomplished as a businessman and as a politician. First, his success as a businessman is well-known. You don't build an empire of businesses unless you have a great talent and intelligence and become a billionaire because of your hard work. This is a minor accomplishment compared to becoming president of the United States. I believe he is the one person in this country of over three hundred million people who could become the president like he did. Just think how he won the Republican primary over seventeen very qualified people. Few people thought he had a chance of winning the Republican primary, then go into the general election, and beat Hillary Clinton who had a political machine backing her. Also, Hillary had eighty-five percent of the liberal media on her side, as well as all liberal Democrats. Then add in the establishment Republicans who were against Trump being the Republican nominee.

Many people thought there was no way for Trump to be elected president. The one big thing working for Trump was that Hillary was a very poor candidate for the Democrats and Obama had done such a poor job as president for eight years, causing the party to be weak. I emphasize that it is a miracle that Mr. Trump was elected president of the United States. He realized that this country was going in the wrong direction and it must be changed. I think he believed he was the person who could change it going in the right direction. Because he loves this country and this country has been so good to him, his choice was to be elected president.

President Trump has a special gift in the way he speaks to his voters, using words that win people to his way of thinking. His facial expression and use of words that most people can understand enabled him to win the election. When he gets up to speak, his body language tells the audience that he is in control and there is specific information he wants to get across to his audience. I have every reason to believe his words have been thought out, even the off-the-cuff remarks and his sense of humor. The liberal Democrats and the media spin his words in a way that is dishonest and give his words a meaning that is different from the true message. When you study and review his speeches, you come up with a very specific point of view that his message is meant to give his audience a specific direction he wants them to go. Democratic policies and politics are not what made this country great. This country is great because the good conservative people took the time to realize what is wrong, then went to the voting booth, and elected a conservative President, a conservative Senate, and a conservative House. In most states, conservative governors were elected, and they also have a majority of conservatives in their Senate and House. In most states, city and county governments are controlled by conservatives. This country is moving in the right direction and will continue in the right direction under the leadership of President Trump.

Many of us agree with President Trump's vision to change Obamacare, build the wall, stop illegal immigration, fix education, move power back to the States, and all the executive orders he has changed for the better, as well as foreign relations with other countries will change for the better. Only a person with President Trump's vision and knowledge can make this happen. I must add, he has the guts and gumption to do whatever it takes to make this happen. At the end of most of these subjects I am writing about, I will end with, What do you think about this? A few months before the presidential election, I sent Donald Trump a contribution for his campaign with a note that says, "Trump will be elected president because he thinks, talks, and acts like a World War II generation person." (See the attached survey of WWII veterans.)

Why did Mr. Trump win the primary election over seventeen very qualified candidates, the liberal news media, and many of the Republican establishment? Previously, I explained Mr. Trump's successful campaign. I just want to add that one of the main reasons he won is that most of the people in this country wanted a change in Washington, DC. President Trump is a very different person in many ways from the previous presidents. President Bush, the younger, was a good president and did many good things for our nation. I would like to clear up one thing—President Bush was not a dummy. Anyone who becomes a US air force pilot must have intelligence and common sense. President Bill Clinton did some good things, but I do not believe he should have been president of the United States. He is a draft dodger, and the way he treats women is beyond respectability of any elected official. I have a hard time finding anything Mr. Obama did that is of lasting good for this country. Obamacare administration was bad: he did great harm to race relations, he did great damage to our foreign relations with most countries, he did great damage to the economy, and he told so many lies you could fill a book with them. I do not hate or wish harm to the Obama and Clinton families; I just want them to go away.

In 2016, we all witnessed as Trump dismantled the myth of Hillary's crooked coronation. He took on the rigged system and won a historic election to become the forty-fifth president of the United States. His promise was to make America safe again by destroying ISIS and securing our borders. He also wanted America working again by repealing terrible job-killing legislation like Obamacare and renegotiating trade deals for American workers. The most spirited and encouraging promise was by standing up for our great country and unleashing the spirit of American exceptionalism. This is one of the omniscient failures of the previous administration by not enthusiastically showing the knowledge and greatness of the American people. Trump shows respect and honor to the greatness of the American people.

If Hillary Clinton had been elected president, I believe this country would have gone in a direction that only liberals would be happy with. I believe she would have appointed liberal Supreme Court justices, which would have caused liberal dogma to come from our court system. This would give us open borders, amnesty for all, proabortion, greater federal control from Washington, DC, and liberal dogma in our public schools. Her vice president, cabinet appointments, and the hundreds or thousands of federal appointments she would made would be liberal. This includes ambassadors to the United Nations as well as ambassadors throughout the world. The thought of Bill Clinton being back in the White House is like a bad dream come true. I can only imagine what it would be like for the next four years or eight years to see and hear what these two would like and say as president. I just thank Jesus that they are out of power and pray never to return to power. Hillary was a very weak candidate to run for president. To this day, it is hard for me to understand why the liberal Democrats would think that an unappealing and dishonest person would be their choice to represent the Democratic Party for president of the United States of America.

One of President Trump's most important assets is the people he has around him. Vice President Pence is the perfect person to support and speak up for President Trump. He is a very likable person who speaks in a strong intelligent way that can be understood by everyone. I believe he is a very loyal person President Trump can count on. I think he chose Mr. Pence because of his qualifications and his character. He could be the person who would follow Mr. Trump as president of the United States. All his cabinet members are outstanding, qualified people who will do a great job in the position they hold. Mr. Trump will appoint great conservative Supreme Court justices.

One of the things that causes Washington, DC, to operate like it does is that all the liberals work for all the lower office holders that turn out all the liberal dogma that is causing the problems in the federal government. President Trump will remove as many of them as possible and replace them with conservatives. President Trump was elected as the outsider to "drain the swamp" of all liberals and disloyal establishment Republicans. Mr. Trump made this promise in his campaign, along with many other promises. I believe he will accomplish most of his promises. The Washington establishment, the liberals, and the media cannot stop him.

Mr. Trump has a very special attitude about people of all races and religions. I believe he will not do anything other than respect and love all people. The thing that stands out in all his speeches is that everything he is doing is for all the people. Mr. Trump has said in many ways that he is more comfortable and at ease with conservative people of all races and religions than with liberals of all races and religions. Another way of saying this is I am more comfortable and at ease with a conservative black person than with a liberal white person.

Republican Candidates

President Trump has said "all politics are local" and suggests ways to support all Republican candidates. Billions of dollars will be invested in the United States by businesses that are encouraged by his economic policies. Together we must grow the Republican "farm team" to support President Trump's conservative agenda in ways large and small. So we must be ready, and we must be prepared to go toe-to-toe with the Democrats who will use every dirty trick in the book to knock us down and derail President Trump's "make America great again" agenda. Together we must fight for the conservative ideals that will restore jobs to our communities, turn around our economy, make our neighborhoods safe, and improve our schools. This means supporting great conservative Republican candidates in our communities every year. Going up against the liberal Democrat fund-raising machine will be tough, but if the 2016 election has taught us anything, it is that you never give up, you never back down, and you never retreat. President Trump sticks to his guns, and most conservative Republican voters agree with this attitude. All the things President Trump promised are in the works, like Attorney General Jeff Sessions has visited the southern border already. He announced new initiatives intended to seriously address illegal immigration. This is in stark contrast to the Obama administration's "prosecutorial discretion." Attorney General Sessions directed federal prosecutors to charge repeat illegal entry offenders with a felony. Illegal immigrants caught with fake documents of IDs will be charged with aggravated identify theft. This new government approach to illegal immigration makes us feel at ease and safe at home, at work, and on our streets and highways.

President Trump's Political Strategy

President Trump's political strategy is to keep the liberals on the defense. His aggressive counterattacks keep the weak leadership in the liberal Democratic Party out of balance and floundering in a way that is fake news and ineffective. Just stop, think, and apply commonsense analysis to liberal Democrats. Just to name a few, Senator Schumer, Nancy Pelosi, Michael Moore, Maxine Waters, Lawrence McDonald, Jesse Jackson, Howard Dean, Chris Matthews, Al Sharpton, Chris Hayes, Rachel Maddow, and Chuck Todd—these people are political hacks and fools. A good definition of a fool is people without knowledge and common sense. To make a stronger case for this definition, fools have poor judgment, are easily deceived, and are easily duped. President Trump has great ability to bring people to his way of thinking and knows how to effectively talk and win most disagreements he has with liberal Democrats. This means he will defeat and win most of the time over the liberal Democrats, which means Mr. Trump is not the normal run-of-the-mill politician. When you try to find the words to define President Trump, it is not easy. A good start would be to say he is brilliant, successful, and a winner. The liberal Democrats can't see and accept the fact that he is a winner and will continue to be a winner. He has defeated the opposition at every turn. They might as well get used to it because I think he will continue to win if he is our president. I think we can look forward to Mr. Trump accomplishing great things for this country.

In his first one hundred days in office, President Trump has shown that his administration's at-home policy and his foreign policy are transparent and very much "America first." His attitude and approach of dealing with the United States Congress is very progressive and straightforward. His agenda (to name a few) is to abolish and redo health care, lower tax rates on business, bring back businesses to the United States, remove all the strict government regulations on business, help the inner-city poor to have jobs and improve their communities, have better foreign relations with all countries, build the southern border wall, and have better control of illegal immigrants back to their home country. What a difference and what a change this would be if President Trump could be successful and make these changes! Living in America would have profound, dramatic change for the better. President Trump says that we should strive to preserve the freedom given to us by God, implemented by our founding fathers, and embodied in the Constitution. We recognize that the traditional family is the strength of our nation. It is our solemn duty to protect life and develop responsible citizens. President Trump understands that the success of our economics depends upon free market principles. If we fail to maintain our sovereignty, we risk losing the freedom to live these ideals. President Trump believes that when we have these feelings and ideas, we have good government.

When President Trump talks about the liberals, it is evident that his language is stated in such a way as to provoke them and put them on the defense. The language they use in return is so harsh, outrageous, and ugly that they are hurting and causing many people to leave the Democratic Party. We witnessed this happening in many states during the 2016 election year. The Republican strategy was to cause the Democrats to go even more overboard with their rhetoric. Mr. Perez, the newly elected chairman of the Democratic Party, said in his acceptance speech that their plan is to fight President Trump in every way to destroy him as president. Anyone observing the politics of the liberal Democrats can see how harsh they are. President Trump's strategy is causing the Democrats to destroy their own party because of the way they are trying to destroy the Republicans. There is every evidence that the strategy of the Republican Party is to move the Democratic Party in the self-destruction of the liberal Democrats. We can only hope that with President Trump's leadership, the Republican Party will be the victor. Earlier in this book, I said I voted for Mr. Trump because he thinks, talks, and acts like the people of the World War II generation. This is a good thing to do for this present generation. I know we all have heard that the WWII generation is the greatest generation. When you study that generation, you learn that there is good reason to say this. People of that generation were very focused on what was happening in the world at that time. They realized that the Nazis and the Fascists were evil empires that had to be destroyed. I think President Trump believes that ISIS and all the other present-day evil empires must be destroyed. You can try meetings and diplomacy and all the known political ways to reach an agreement, but it is a waste of time. You try to work with evil governments like the Nazis, Fascists, and ISIS but finally realize there is just one way to deal with them and that is to defeat and destroy them into an unconditional surrender.

When you study the WWII generation, you can see why we won that war. Our government did not make the war political. There was just one policy—do whatever you must to defeat and destroy the enemy. The government at that time, both Democrats and Republicans, must be loyal to the military and work together to win. This is what President Trump is trying to do today. The big problem is that the liberal Democrats are doing everything they can to destroy President Trump. This is not just hearsay because many liberal Democrats have said this in television, radio, and writing. I believe President Trump is a strong-enough leader to overcome the liberal media and the liberal Republicans that are so against President Trump. With the help of all the good people who support President Trump and with his great leadership ability, he will always win. When studying the WWII generation, most people observe that they have common sense, are honest, accept personal responsibility, and are very loyal to the United States. Most young men were ready and willing to serve in the military. I think most people at that time loved this country and wanted to keep it free. As our leader, President Trump is trying to encourage everyone to love this country and support its government.

President Trump's Income Tax Return

I understand why President Trump does not want to release his income tax return information. Have you noticed what happens to people who release their tax information to the public, especially people who have been very successful with various business interests? They are philanthropic people who give large amounts of gifts to charities, religious organizations, political parties, politicians, etc. These donations are tax-deductible. Those who are critical and complaining then review those tax returns. Many of them are dishonest, and they nitpick every little tax-deduction to the point of ridiculousness. They foolishly investigate and may discover minor discrepancies and make a big deal out of it. President Trump is bound to have a long and complicated tax return. He knows how the liberal media and liberal Democrats would be dishonest about the way they spin every little detail about his tax information. So why bother to give them tax information that they will make public?

Russia

Much has been said about President Trump and his relationship with Russia. There is no evidence that anyone in the Trump administration has had any illegal contact with the Russians. Liberal Democrats are so out of touch with the truth and grasping for anything to make Republicans look bad.

President Trump and Prime Minister Vladimir Putin have a very unusual relationship. They seem to respect each other and want to work together for better relations. I think they both realize this would be good for both countries. It would help with trade and commerce, which would help both economies with trading products that each may want and need. One of the problems with President Trump and Prime Minister Putin is that most government officials of the United States do not trust Putin. In fact, most government officials of this country believe that Putin is doing everything possible to undermine the United States. Putin is doing great harm to the United States relative to Middle Eastern countries: Iraq, Iran, Syria, and all other countries in that area. Putin invaded Ukraine and took ownership of part of Ukraine. He has also taken many people prisoner in that country. One of the most outrageous things Putin has done is interfere with our 2016 presidential election. Putin was known to hate Hillary Clinton and wanted Trump to win the election. It is considered by the FBI and CIA that Russia had very little effect on our 2016 presidential election. Democrats disagree with the FBI and CIA and believe Russia caused Trump to win the election.

President Trump has the right attitude about dealing with Putin. President Trump has been excellent in dealmaking all his life. He thinks it is better to try and have good diplomatic relations with Putin than to start out with a hard-line approach. Most politicians and many who follow politics say to try to improve our diplomatic relations with Russia would be a good thing. Christopher Caldwell has some interesting information about how Americans and President Trump think of Putin. But he suggests all people are capable of making up their own mind but rather how to understand Putin. Putin did not come out of nowhere. The Russian people not only tolerate him; they revere him. You can get a better idea of why he has ruled for seventeen years if you remember that within a few years of Communism's fall, average life expectancy in Russia had fallen below that of Bangladesh. Under the leadership of Putin, it has improved quite a bit. There are two things Putin did that cemented the loyalty of Solzhenitsyn and other Russians—he restrained the billionaires who were looting the country, and he restored Russia's standing abroad. When Putin took power in 1999–2000, his country was defenseless. It was bankrupt, and it was being carved up by its new kleptocratic elites in collusion with its odd imperial rivals, the Americans. Putin changed that. In the first decade of this century, he did what Kemal Ataturk had done in Turkey in 1920. Out of a crumbling empire, he rescued a nation-state and gave it coherence and purpose.

But anyone who has read the public documentation on what the claim was will find only speculation and arguments from authority and attempt to make repetition do the work of logic. "Most Russians have come to believe that democracy is what happened in their country between 1990 and 2000, and they do not want any more of it." Vladimir Putin is not today's biggest threat to the United States. So why are people thinking about Putin as much as they do? Because he has become a symbol of national self-determination. Populist conservatives see him the way progressives once saw Fidel Castro as the one person who said he wouldn't submit to the world that surrounds him. You didn't have to be a communist to appreciate the way Castro, regardless of his excuses, was carving out a space of autonomy for his country. In the same way, Putin's conduct is bound to win sympathy even from some Russian enemies, the men who feel the international system is not delivering for them. Generally, if you like that system, you will consider Vladimir Putin a menace. If you don't like it, you will have some sympathy for him. Putin has become a symbol of national sovereignty in the battle with globalism. That turns out to be the big battle of our time. Our last election shows that is true, even here. Obama caused Vladimir Putin to become more powerful over the last eight years, as well as a lot of other organizations.

Trump and People of Other Ethnicities

Mr. Trump respects and admires the Asian culture, that is, their family structure, their children getting a good education, their job skills, and how the Asians came to this country and accept the American culture. Trump always adds that he would encourage all nationalities to blend in and become Americanized as the Asian people.

Another group of people that President Trump admires and respects is the Jewish people. He believes that the United States and Israel share a special, long-standing relationship based on shared values, a mutual commitment to a republican form of government and a strategic alliance that benefits both nations. Our foreign policy with Israel should reflect the right of sovereign nations to govern themselves and have self-determination. Our policy is inspired by God's biblical promise to bless those who bless Israel and curse those who curse Israel, and we further invite other nations and organizations to enjoy the benefits of that promise. President Trump is telling Israel and the rest of the world, and especially the politicians of the United States, that our foreign policy is freedom for all nations. The Trump administration will lead boldly up front, not like the last administration leading from behind. President Trump showed this kind of leadership in the missile strike on the air base in Syria.

Liberal Democrats

President Trump's attitude toward the establishment and liberals is very straightforward and direct. He knows they are very mad and upset about losing the election. He wisely takes advantage of this weakness. He attacks all the wrong things they have done.

Democrats are very much on the defensive. The liberal Democratic Party will continue to decline and be less relative because of their leadership such as Schumer and Pelosi. The voices we mainly hear representing the liberal Democratic Party are Michael Moore, Bill Marr, Maxine Waters, Rosie O'Donnell, Jesse Jackson, and Al Sharpton. When people like them are your main spokesmen and they are fanatic liberal Democrats, you can go only one way—down and less important than commonsense people who are politically active and vote in all elections.

Every day, more people see the way the liberal Democratic Party is going. They realize how out of touch they are with the normal, common sense people. They see through the crazy, foolish agenda of the liberal Democrats. As a result, thousands of people are moving to the conservative Republican Party. Because of the strong leadership of President Trump, the Democrats will become a more minority party. There are many reasons for this to happen: the failure of Obamacare, doubling the national debt, additional people receiving food stamps, problematic foreign relations with other countries, race relations worse than ever before, little resolved about inner-city poverty, immigration/amnesty problems (very little has been done to stop illegals from crossing the southern border), and the military gutted so much that it is less powerful than any time after WWII. The economy and all the regulations have hurt business and hurt the IRS and Justice Departments as well as well as many other government agencies. I could give many more examples of how much Obama hurt this country. With President Trump in office and in control of the Executive Branch, and the Republicans in control of both houses and the Supreme Court, more inside information will come out about Obama's eight years in office that could be damaging to this country.

Liberal Democrats are so out of touch with the truth and are grasping for anything to make Republicans look bad. They are at the lowest level of approval by voters in this country since the 1920s. President Trump knows why this is true. The Democrat policies and politics did not work in the Obama administration and will not work today. Leadership of the Democratic Party is almost nonexistent. With the poor leadership and people like Michael Moore, Maher, Waters, Jackson, Dean, O'Donnell, and Sharpton, who are so radical and liberal, very few voters want them to lead this country. The Trump administration realizes that what they are saying are outrageous, horrendous, ugly lies, so the right thing to do is let them go with this rhetoric. They are hurting the Democratic Party in ways that all voters can see. The Democrat politics will not make this country work in the way of freedom and giving the people a true democracy, which we deserve. All these people who are so strongly against President Trump will have egg on their face because he will accomplish all the things he promised and more. Before he completes his eight years as president, he will have made this country great again.

Obama's Shadow Government

President Trump realizes that Obama is setting up a shadow government where he lives, in Washington, DC. Obama is the only past president to remain in Washington, DC, in recent years. Woodrow Wilson is the only other former president to remain in the city. Obama is doing this to protect his legacy. He will be doing everything he can to hurt the Trump administration. He has already started leaking bad information about the Trump administration. For example, in his last few months in office, he made it easier for the Justice Department to give out information about the department that would make his administration look good. It has been widely reported in news stories that Obama held over many people from his presidential staff to do research and check on the Trump administration in every possible way. Then they leak it to the news media. No ex-president has ever done these kinds of things to his successor. The Trump administration thinks the reason Obama is doing this is for revenge because of the derogatory things that have been said about him. Also, Obama was greatly upset because Hillary Clinton lost the election. Obama has stated that Trump is unqualified to be president and he would lead this country in the wrong direction and be a complete disaster for the United States. The Democrats thought Hillary would win the election in a landslide. They also thought that Trump's winning was a fraud. The Trump administration realizes what the Obama people are trying to do and will expose and defeat them. The liberal Democrats are in a panic and unhinged. The Democratic leadership, Schumer and Pelosi, are not real leaders, and their persona is unfriendly and dark. This means the liberal Democratic Party will be less of a political power in the future.

Organizing for Action

President Trump's team should do everything possible to expose and destroy Organizing for Action because it is a strong organization that can cause destruction and harm to the president's agenda. Former US representative Bob Edgar (D-Penn.) sounded the alarm about Organizing for Action in 2013, suggesting the group was dangerous to democracy. If Obama is serious about his often-expressed desire to rein in big money in politics, he should disavow Organizing for Action and any plan to schedule regular meetings with its major donors. Obama, with his shadow presidency organization operating within his Washington, DC, offices, should remove himself from contact with this fanatic, activist, liberal group of radical people.

Radicalism

It is the fanatics like radical Muslims, Communists, Fascists, and Nazis that rule a lot of the world at this time in history. It is the fanatics who march. It is the fanatics who wage any one of fifty wars worldwide. It is the fanatics who systematically slaughter Christians or tribal groups throughout Africa and are gradually taking over the entire continents in a terrorist wave of force. It was the fanatics who bomb, behead, murder, or "honor kill." It is the fanatics who take over mosque after mosque. It is the fanatics who zealously spread the stoning and hanging of rape victims and homosexuals. It is the fanatics who teach their young to kill and to become suicide bombers. The most fanatic of these atrocious acts is the poison gassing of children. President Trump is aware of these fanatic acts of evil and the nations that committed them. He has said they must be stopped. He has already taken action in that direction with the missile attack on Syria.

Voter Fraud

Voter fraud is a very real thing that is happening in this country. President Trump has brought voter fraud to the attention of the voting public. They have been concerned about this for many years. He hopes that all future elections will be more strict about who can vote. He believes each voter should have a personal ID card. Mr. Trump sees what changes need to be made, and then he goes to the public with a plan to make it happen. Because President Trump has made a big issue of voter fraud, we should have more honest elections in the future. Most people want fair, honest elections. President Trump brought up this very important issue to encourage all eligible voters to get involved and vote in their local elections.

The Obama-Holder Department of Justice refused to pursue the New Black Panther Party. The group was caught on tape committing felonies by attempting to intimidate Caucasian voters into staying away from the polls. Black Panthers have been caught on tape calling for the murder of white people and their babies. A president who would let this kind of activity go on is unacceptable to be president of the United States. Meanwhile, as Obama has refused to enforce immigration law, the result is chaos.

Education

President Trump says the informed and right-thinking people are conservative voters who always vote for Republican candidates. This group of voters acknowledge that the education of children is primarily the responsibility of the parents or guardians. The role of the government is to help facilitate that responsibility. Parents have the right to withdraw their child from any specialized program. Government should urge the legislature to enact penalties for violation of parental rights. Parents and legal guardians may choose to educate their children in private schools to include, but not limited to, home schools and parochial schools without government interference, through definition, regulations, accreditation, licensing, or testing. Government should recognize parental responsibility and authority regarding sex education. Parents must be given an opportunity to review the material prior to giving their consent.

Election Laws

President Trump supports modification and strengthening of election laws to ensure ballot integrity and fair elections. He supports repeal of all motor voter laws registering voters every four years, requiring voter ID, proof of residency and citizenship, retention of the thirty-day registration deadline, and requiring that a list of certified deaths be provided to the government so the names of the deceased are removed from the list of registered voters. President Trump strongly believes that the 2016 election year had many thousands of illegal immigrants voting and people using information of dead people to vote. There is no doubt that the 2016 election year had many fraud voters because many state voter organizations did a survey that showed this to be true. Voter fraud in this country is a big problem for all who want honesty in our government. Mr. Trump made a big deal out of voter fraud when he was campaigning against Hillary. Hillary and the Democrats were trying to promote voter fraud within the illegal immigration population by attempting to pass laws so immigrants could vote. President Trump's advice to all legal voters is to be actively involved in all elections and make sure they are honest elections.

Judicial Restraint

President Trump urges Congress to adopt a Constitutional Restoration Act and support the principle of judicial restraint, which requires judges to interpret and apply rather than make the law. He supports judges who strictly interpret the law based on intent. He opposes judges who assume for themselves legislative powers. He calls on Congress and the Senate to use their constitutional powers to restrain activist judges.

Foreign Relations

The present administration must deal with foreign relations with countries all over the world. The Obama administration had bad relations with most of the countries in the world. Most countries did not trust Obama to keep his word. So many times, he made promises he did not keep, like the redline he drew in Syria. Also, most of the countries in the Middle East know how he cut back on the military budget, which made a weaker military. The biggest mistake Obama made was to pull all troops out of Iraq. After the Iraq pullout, the radical Muslims moved in and gave birth to ISIS radicals.

As President Trump has said, he inherited a big mess. The president has talented people working with him, and he has leadership skills, so they will have the background and wisdom to solve most of the foreign relations problems. This will not be easy because of the different cultures around the world. One of the most important reasons foreign countries will fall in line with the United States is because President Trump plans to build up our military to be the most modern and strongest in the world. All countries will see what the president has done and will want to be a partner with a winner!

Israel and Obama had a distant (cool) and fractured relationship. I think it is reasonable to say they did not respect each other. When you saw them together on television, they appeared to be uncomfortable with one another. From his speech and actions, Obama seemed to support the Palestinians more than Israel. In Israel's last election, Obama supported Netanyahu's rival with money and sent people from Obama's personal staff to help run his rival's campaign. In his first month in office, President Trump had a meeting with Netanyahu in Washington, DC. They had a very cordial, successful meeting. President Trump assured Netanyahu that the United

States and Israel are allies. If Israel is attacked by an enemy nation, the United States will be there to fight side by side. Mr. Trump said he will be meeting with the Palestinian leadership in the future and hopes to arrange a meeting with Israel and the Palestinians. President Trump has said he believes he can negotiate a treaty with Israel and Palestine that will lead to peace between the two nations.

According to one recent survey, 81 percent of Russians now have a negative view of the United States. That is much higher than at the end of the Cold War era. This means in the last eight years, the Obama administration did a poor job of foreign relations with the Russians. Hillary Clinton had a lot to do with these bad relations when she was secretary of state. She pushed the Reset button with Russia and then did not keep her promises. Obama trashed George W. Bush's policy toward Vladimir Putin, while promising a new reset approach (illustrated with a plastic red button) to an aggressive dictator raised few eyebrows at the time. Nor did many Americans worry that our Pacific allies were upset over Chinese and North Korean aggression that seemed to ignore US deterrence. On the other hand, President Trump believes with the correct approach and making the right deals, we could have a much better and friendlier relationship with Russia. With the leadership and deal-making of the president and the new secretary of state Tillerson, who has much experience at dealing with foreign countries, we should have a better working relationship with Russia. One thing needs to be cleared up—the accusation that Russia tried to influence our 2016 presidential election. Supposedly, Russia preferred Trump over Clinton to be our president. The FBI and CIA and other government agencies say Russian collusion is not true. Russia has also strongly stated that they did not influence the US election.

Relations between Mexico and the United States is strained, to say the least. Mexico thinks President Trump is too hard on them regarding amnesty with illegal immigrants in this country. Mexico disagrees with President Trump about Mexico paying for *the wall*. The wall along the southern border is one of Mr. Trump's most important promises, and it must be kept. The construction of the wall must be started soon. He realizes that most people are opposed to all illegal immigrants coming into this country. On the other hand, we are not opposed to legal immigrants coming here. The rule that must be applied is that all immigrants must be vetted as completely as possible. President Trump realizes that many illegal immigrants are lawbreakers. In the first month of Trump's administration, a more aggressive effort has been made to deport criminal aliens. The Trump administration has added people and money to the border patrol budget. With this new budget and building the southern border wall, we'll do a better job of keeping them from getting back into this country. This administration is in favor of enforcing the sanctuary city federal law that applies to criminals who have been deported.

If that criminal is caught back in the United States, he or she will be sent to prison. The president and most people will do whatever is necessary to keep drugs and criminals out of this country. This may require much-tougher law enforcement to make America safe.

Mexico wants US factories to move to Mexico, but our country will put a larger import tax on much of the products manufactured in Mexico and shipped to the United States. There are many other things that Mexico and the United States disagree on. President Trump's agenda is to say it in a few words, always putting America first. This plainly says when it comes to a relationship with any other country, it will always be what is good for America.

How well President Trump deals with Russia, Iran, Syria, and North Korea will be a big factor in how successful his foreign policy will be. Trump will be out front and on offense with his leadership abilities, not like Obama, who led from behind and caused all the foreign policy problems that President Trump will have to correct. President Trump has assured the people who elected him president that he will govern according to the limits and powers the US Constitution gives the president, not like Obama, who arbitrarily declared an existing law unconstitutional and refused to enforce it. President Trump is already producing positive results with many foreign countries. All people of the United States can rest assured that President Trump will continue with positive results with all foreign nations of the world by working together to make this a better world. The president knows the Democrats will be out in full force this year to fight us at every turn.

ISIS and Terrorists

The Obama administration did very little to control or defeat ISIS and all the other radical Muslim terrorists. In fact, they added to their numbers and spread to most of the countries in the Middle East. Obama did very little about the terrorist acts committed in this country. President Trump said Obama just played along with the terrorists in a way that gave them courage to continue their terrorist acts. Obama was doing just enough to keep people satisfied with his action to stay in the president's office until his term of eight years was over. He did not have the courage to do what was necessary to defeat and destroy the terrorists. Obama was aware of what he was doing—just leave it up to the next president to do what should have been done to destroy terrorists. Mr. Trump said during the primary campaign that he would defeat and destroy terrorists. When he was running for president against Hillary Clinton, he said the same thing. In his first few days in office, he met with his military generals and told them to draw up a plan to defeat the terrorists. The generals have made that plan and have started to execute it by sending marines into Syria to defeat ISIS. President Trump will continue his military plan until he destroys and defeats the terrorists. His plan is to build up our military forces and make them stronger than ever before in the history of this nation. President Trump will do whatever needs to be done to win.

Under the Obama administration, our allies got the message that there are few consequences to aggression and neutrals that joining with America does not mean ending up on the winning side. The result is that the Middle East we have known since the end of World War II is no longer with us.

Protesters/Demonstrators

I agree with the way President Trump responds to protesters in the streets, on campuses, and the others who attack him in many dishonest ways. I believe he has the right to respond to the attacks, and he usually wins the argument. I have watched the news media many years. Most of them are dishonest and biased toward the president and all conservatives. Not only are their words dishonest and biased, but the expression in their face and their body language is obvious when they give the news. The media is 90 percent liberal with their talk and their money. They give 90 percent to liberal political parties. It is difficult to understand how the people who own the radio, television, and written word news organizations let the people who work for them be so biased and dishonest. Some of them are mean, ugly, evil, and hateful to conservatives. Beyond the pale is 80 to 90 percent of what they report. President Trump understands how all these liberals operate and what they are trying to do. With his wisdom and intelligence, he defeated them in the primary election and the general election, and he is defeating them in every way now that he is president.

Fake/Fraud News

Mr. Trump has exposed the fake news to all the people who want to know what is going on in this country. This fake news needs to be exposed for many good reasons. Many people who were watching fake news took it for granted that this dishonest information was true. Now that fake news has been exposed, many people realize how biased and misleading it is. This is just another way President Trump has shown how knowledgeable and in touch he is. I think he realizes how much fake news the previous administration had given out for the last eight years. His simple straightforward way of talking to people is one of his great personal assets. This country is now aware of fake news and is made aware to check the news in and out, up and down. This is what this administration wants people to do—must do. The reason the president wants us to do this is his agenda is the right agenda to make this country great again. This administration wants us to check out what the news stations are saying and check out the character of the people reporting the news. Use your common sense, and think through what they say. Don't fall for the spin and dishonest way the liberals present the news. President Trump uses the words "common sense" on purpose and for a good reason.

Liberal CNN and MSNBC, along with all the other mainstream media people who hate President Trump, will be giving the news reports. These people are not journalists or news reporters; they are commentators who spin their news programs to always place President Trump in a dark, ugly bad way. A total of eighty-five percent of media people do not like Republicans or their conservative agenda, and eighty-five percent of the liberal media vote for Democrats and give campaign money to the Democrats. This kind of information shows just how wrong the liberals can be. Liberals support sanctuary cities that harbor immigration criminals who murder innocent citizens and murder their own people.

Fake news has caused great harm to the United States. It has caused mistrust of government, politicians, and the news media. Just think how serious the above statement is when you don't know whom to believe or trust. It doesn't get any more serious than this when our people are dealing with this kind of information every day. All of us should accept the responsibility of being more knowledgeable about our government, politicians, and news media and hold them accountable. When President Trump talks about cable news, he says there are only two television networks that are fair and balanced—Fox and One America News. Most of the time, their people, who report the news, are intelligent and knowledgeable and try to be fair in telling the stories they are reporting on. Most of the time, they tell both sides of the story and let listeners decide what to believe. When they misreport a story, they apologize and correct their errors in a calm, direct way. One of the good things about Fox and One America News is that they do not think they know it all and talk down to their viewers. All the statements said about Fox and One America News do not apply to the other cable news stations and the drive-by or mainstream news networks. The mainstream media has an attitude of partisanship—we know what you need to see and hear. One commentator on MSNBC said that their job was to tell us how and what to think. The Trump administration understands what the fake news media is doing. President Trump likes a good fight and is doing what he should do.

He answers all attacks with a strong counterattack. Most people in this country think the president is doing the right thing by attacking right back and hitting them harder than they hit him. This administration is doing what most people wanted—call out and expose the fake news people for what they really are. His approach is strong and simple—hit back quickly and hit hard. His method is straightforward and doesn't pull any punches. He is exposing the fake media for all to see what they really are. Fox News has by far the highest-rated news show of any network. They honestly try to be fair and balanced and unafraid.

All the fraud media news shows have one thing in common—they are all liberal in every way. President Trump has surprised almost everyone with his conservative agenda over very little liberal agenda. He does not just sit back and take these attacks. Most of the time, he attacks back. If you follow the news closely, you know when they attack him, and he attacks them in return. Most of the time when the dust settles, both sides have given their points of view, and the attack ends. Most of the time, President Trump beats down the attacker and wins.

Fraud news media is very much against President Trump's agenda. A Harvard University survey proves that over 90 percent of the fake news about President Trump is *negative*. It is the truth to say that 85 percent of the fraud news media personally dislikes or hates President Trump. In much of their reporting on radio and television programs, many of them say very violent and ugly things about the president. To name a few, here are some fake news people:

- *Chuck Todd*, MSNBC, has a very nervous smile on his face that comes across in a way that he is not telling the truth.
- *Chris Matthews*, MSNBC, insults and talks over people so much that you can't hear what either of them is saying.
- *Don Lemon*, CNN, always manages some way, somehow to work racism into any subject they are discussing.
- *Rachel Maddow*, MSNBC, is very obnoxious to hear and watch. When she talks, she grins, laughs, makes silly faces, and wiggles around her chair. Nearly everything she says is very negative about the present administration. Rachel comes across as thinking she is the smartest, cutest person you listen to, so just sit there, listen, and do what I tell you. Then you will have all the news that is important for you to know.
- *Anderson Cooper*, CNN, does not say a lot of negative things about Mr. Trump, but he asks a lot of negative questions of his guests; and then he lets them say whatever ugly things they want to. He never corrects them, especially when they are attacking President Trump.

- *Chris Hayes*, MSNBC. His show is very amateurish with shallow depth of information. Most of his guests are not very well-known in the news world. Other than that, what I said about Anderson Cooper applies to Chris Hayes.
- *Erin Burnett*, CNN. Her show is very lightweight and gives little hard news. Other than that, what I said about Anderson Cooper applies to Erin.
- *Lawrence O'Donnell*, MSNBC His show is hard to describe without using dirty language. He is the most foulmouthed, obnoxious person on television. His one-hour show, from beginning to end, is vicious slander, attacking the president. The expression on his face during the entire show is a contemptuous smirk about President Trump. Every guest on his program belittles and attacks the president. It is hard to understand why anyone would produce his show. Also, it is hard to understand why anyone would advertise their products on his show.

Political Appointees

The Trump administration's political appointments have been one of their most outstanding achievements. No president before Mr. Trump has gone out into the private sector and recruited so many successful business professionals to serve in their administration. Most presidents have appointed existing political people who are personal friends. They have proven to be successful in many lines of business. These appointees have expertise in fields of work that can only be helpful to President Trump. When you have this much brainpower on your staff, it means you will be able to attack government problems in many ways. When your staff is made up of establishment politicians, they end up trying to solve problems the way they have always done it. They are slow to change. The Trump administration has already made significant changes in the way the federal government operates. President Trump is very different from past presidents in the way he governs Washington, DC, establishment politicians, and they are having a hard time accepting and understanding Mr. Trump. It does not matter what the establishment thinks or does.

If he is successful in passing all his agenda and turning this country in the right direction, he will win over the majority of people. This would mean he will be president for eight years. He will accomplish all his campaign promises and make this country great again. Mr. Trump will win over the Washington, DC, establishment.

Health Care: "Obamacare"

Another promise the president has in the works with his administration is repeal of Obamacare. Obamacare is a disaster that in time will explode and cease to exist. The premiums and deductibles are so costly that people cannot afford them. Also, insurance companies do not want to be in the insurance business in many states because they cannot make a profit. In some states, there is only one insurance producer. President Trump's health-care plan will cut the cost of insurance premiums and provide better health care. The president has, in the works, better health care for veterans' hospitals.

When Obama was trying to get Obamacare passed and made into the law of the land, he told many lies about it. He said, "You can keep the doctor you have." He also said, "You can keep the insurance plan you now have." This will be Obama's legacy—he was the most dishonest president to hold that office.

Obamacare has failed in many ways, that is:

1. Costs have gone up on an average of 25 percent and 100 percent in one state.
2. He falsely promised you could keep your doctor.
3. He falsely promised you could keep your present health-care plan.
4. Many doctors will not treat some patients on Obamacare.
5. Many hospitals will not accept some patients on Obamacare.
6. Many people who do not have any insurance end up going to public hospital emergency rooms. That is the most expensive health care of all. This means your tax dollars are paying for those who go there.

Obamacare and the Democrats believe health care is a right, not a privilege reserved for those who are able to pay for it. Every family deserves health care they can depend on and a system that ensures stability, security, and access to care. Democrats support the right of a woman to acquire contraception or other reproductive services through her health insurance provider that may not be impinged or abridged by an employee for any reason or can be terminated or subjected to any form of harassment or retaliation by her employer related to any health-care choices. They support family planning funding for pregnancy prevention and preventive health care by all qualified providers in regulated, licensed medical facilities rather than biased and nonmedical activities in centers that are deceptive and unregulated.

Republicans believe health-care decisions should be between a patient and a health-care professional and should be protected from government intrusion. We urge the passage of health-care reform that results in more affordable health care through a market-based, competitive, and transparent health-care system, including care reform, interstate competition, general accountability, and oversight. But who cared that the Obama Affordable Care Act was 2,500 pages long? He has made it impossible for Americans to keep their individual or employee-sponsored group health insurance. Too few seemed to care that almost everything the president had promised about Obamacare—keep your health plan, retain your doctor, save money on your premiums, sign up easily online—while we were lowering the annual deficit and reducing medical expenditures, was an object lie. Among presidents in modern US history, Obama has been a uniquely divisive force. It began with his forcing Obamacare through Congress—the only major legislation in US history to be passed with no votes from the opposition party.

Veterans/Military/First Responders

In speeches and debates, Mr. Trump has pointed out how little the establishment and liberals have done for the military, how they promised to help people in poverty in the inner-city neighborhoods, and how little they have helped. The Obama administration did great harm to this. They have given little support to the police and border personnel.

President Trump has made it very clear that the United States will no longer stand down and let aggressive countries commit their atrocities against another nation. This was the attitude of the WWII generation. President Trump will keep these attitudes and beliefs as long as he is our president. One of President Trump's promises was to be transparent and keep us informed about foreign relations with other nations. He will not do like the Obama administration did and tell foreign leaders in advance what action he planned against them. President Trump said he will always keep his word about what action he plans to take. The president and his advisers will keep all planned actions against other nations secret until he is ready to proceed. Totalitarian, aggressive nations that are bullies and tyrants only respect toughness and strength, like Germany and Japan before WWII. There is just one answer to nations that take this approach to their foreign policy—"defeat and destroy them."

One of the most important things the Trump administration is doing is strongly supporting veterans, police officers, and active-duty military. Before I go into how they are supporting these organizations, please think long and hard about how important these organizations are to us and to this country. What would it be like without them? In most of President Trump's public speeches, he gives praise to veterans, police officers, and the active military. To most people, it does not get any more important than this. When he mentions these organizations, he goes into detail, such as veterans deserve the best medical care. If they do not get this medical care at the veterans' hospitals, they should be given a voucher to any private hospital they choose. President Trump has a plan to make all branches of active military the strongest in the world. Foreign enemies do not attack the strong, only the weak. This is common sense. He tries to get the public to understand what a hard job the police have. We can only do our very best to understand what it is like to put your life on the line and deal with murderers, robbers, and sexual abusers, serve a warrant, break up fights, and withstand verbal and physical abuse from those kinds of people. You must be a very special person to give your life to this hard work.

His plan is to provide much better care and make sure veterans do not have to wait a long time to get an appointment for medical treatment. If he does not get an appointment in a reasonable amount of time, he will be given the option of going to a private hospital, and the federal government will pay for his treatment. President Trump has made it very clear how he feels about veterans and active military. His agenda is to improve both veteran and active military personnel benefits in every way and give them better care than ever before. The president has already given the pentagon orders to add to and improve all branches of our military.

President Trump treats veterans more special and important than the average everyday citizen, especially those who serve in combat and have a special attitude of patriotic love for this country. Mr. Trump will be doing everything he can to pass legislation that will make sure the veterans at all veterans' hospitals are treated fairly. He is already passing executive orders to build up all branches of our military. He will continue this buildup until the US military is back to full strength like it was after WWII. He believes that a strong military is what keeps the peace and prevents acts of war. President Trump knows that the US military is at the same level it was just after WWI. He believes this country has been treated with contempt by many progressive nations that are on the move against other countries and by military forces invading other nation's territory by military force.

Also, the reason this is happening is because the president would not militarily cross his redline and stop Syria's use of poison gas on its own people or do anything about Russia's invasion of Ukraine and taking their territory by military force.

Barack Obama: Personal

Obama made a surprising remark at a White House Christmas party, telling Fox News that he was "the most powerful man in the world." Obama appears to be a tormented man filled with resentment, anger, and disdain for anyone with a different opinion or view than his. He acts in the most hateful, spiteful, malevolent, vindictive ways to manipulate and maintain power and control over others. Perhaps, because he grew up as a child harboring an abiding bitterness toward the United States that was instilled in him by his family and mentors, it seems to have never left him. Obama's background as a child, teenager, and adult is very different from most Americans. Most American children sing our patriotic songs in kindergarten and do normal teenage activities. We know very little about Obama's unusual college days.

Obama doesn't delight in being part of America and its greatness. Rather, he was separated from these experiences and doesn't really understand us and what it means to be an American. His background and upbringing is so different from most Americans. His white mother was very liberal, and his black father was considered to be a liberal Communist.

His childhood was mostly spent in Africa. His teenage years were divided between his mother's parents in Hawaii. His young years growing up were different from most Americans. There are a lot of questions about Obama, his life, background from his early childhood, up to when he was elected president of the United States. Think about this: Where are Obama's past girlfriends? You would think there would be at least one. But no past girlfriend popped up anywhere. This is really weird! We have a lot of background of the other presidents.

Have you ever wondered why no one ever came forward from Obama's past, saying they knew him, attended school with him, were his friend, etc.? Has anyone talked to his professors? Isn't it odd that no one is bragging that they knew him or taught him or lived with him? George Stephanopoulos, ABC News, said the same thing during the 2008 campaign. Even George questioned why no one has acknowledged that the president was in their classroom or ate in the same cafeteria or made impromptu speeches on campus. Stephanopoulos was a schoolmate of Obama at Columbia, class of 1984. He said he never had a single class with him. Since he is such a great orator, why doesn't anyone in Obama's college class remember him? Why won't he allow Columbia to release his records? Do you, like millions of others, assume all of this is explainable even though no one has? His photograph does not appear in the school yearbook. Fox News contacted four hundred Columbia University students from the period when Obama claims to have been there, but not one remembers him. For example, Wayne Allyn Root was (like Obama) a political science major at Columbia who graduated in 1983. In 2008, Root says of Obama, "I don't know a single person at Columbia that knew him and they all know me. I don't have a single classmate who ever knew Barack Obama at Columbia." Root adds that he was "Class of '83 political science, pre-law and you don't get more exact or closer than that. Never met him in my life. Don't know anyone who ever met him." Obama's photograph does not appear in the school yearbook and Obama consistently declines requests to talk about his years at Columbia, provide school records, or provide the name of any former classmates or friends while at Columbia. Then there were Obama's experiences in Chicago as a community organizer. When you look at Obama's background, you can understand why he does not think or act like the average American citizen. He seldom shows respect for our great history or speak lovingly of the United States or its people. Most Americans have great pride and love for this country. Obama does not really understand us and what it means to be an American. No other president has used such tactics to harm and hurt the people of this country.

Obama sat for twenty years in a Liberation Theology Church condemning Christianity and professing Marxism. Obama said we need to have a conversation about race in America. Fair enough, but this time, it must be a two-way conversation. White America needs to be heard from, not just lectured to. This time, the silent majority needs to have its say.

It has been circulating that according to the US census, there is only one Barack Obama but twenty-seven Social Security numbers and over eighty aliases. When people think about Obama and who he really is, how he feels about America and all the people, the only conclusion many people have is that he is a very strange and difficult person to understand. He is the most unqualified, inexperienced president this country has ever had. In his eight years as president, Obama did great harm to America. He left a great big mess that President Trump will have to clean up.

Barack Obama: The Politician

Obama left America with a debt problem and a failure of leadership. Americans deserve better. If you have no debt and have ten dollars in your wallet, you are wealthier than 25 percent of all Americans. Because of leadership failures, the Obama administration could not pay its own bills. It is a sign that we now depend on ongoing financial assistance from foreign countries to finance our government's reckless fiscal policies. United States' debt weakens us domestically and internationally. Leadership means that "the buck stops here." Instead, Washington is shifting the burden of bad choices onto the backs of our children and grandchildren. The reason US government does not have a lot of tax monies paid into the Treasury is that almost half or 47 percent of all Americans do not put a single penny out of their paychecks into savings. Also, many people are not honest about paying the taxes they owe. Obama likewise has done some crazy things that seemed for years to have no ramifications. Unfortunately, typical of the ways of Nemesis (a bitter goddess who waits until the opportune moment to demand payment for past misdeeds), suddenly, the bills for Obama's eight years of folly are coming due for the American people. Al Sharpton would be America's greatest at-large criminal if not for Hilleary's tens of millions swapped for influence and favors. Sharpton owes nearly $5 million in delinquent taxes to IRS and New York State. Also, the Federal Election Commission forced him to return $100,000 in taxpayer money provided by FEC. One of many abuses was his $145,146 charge for campaign letter preparation at Kinko's. Later, FEC fined Sharpton $275,000. This is an example of how many people avoid taxes and cause our government to be at a loss with debt limit.

Obama had no method of paying for the US big debt other than printing more money, thereby surreptitiously taxing everyone through inflation, including the poor he claims to be helping and cheapening the dollar to the point that some countries are talking another reserve currency and saddling the next generation with enormous debts. A lot of this debt is because Obama gave money to foreign countries wastefully, like giving $100 million in US Treasury funds to rebuild foreign mosques. Obama exempted Muslims from penalties under Obamacare that the rest of us must pay. Obama's Internal Revenue Service used its unparalleled power to stymie political dissent. No one has been held accountable. Obama threw the support of his administration behind the building of the Ground Zero "victory mosque" overlooking the hallowed crater of the World Trade Center.

One wonders if there is a remaining ally nation that trusts Obama. And worse, no American enemy fears him. Even now, Democratic allies no longer trust America. Obama has alienated our most important and longest-standing Arab allies—Egypt and Saudi Arabia. Anti-Iran Arab states have lost respect for him. Virtually nothing Obama has done has left America or the world better since he became president. Most everything he has touched has been made worse.

Obama's ambassadors to Libya and three other Americans were murdered by terrorists in Benghazi, Libya. No one has been blamed. The only blame the Obama administration leveled was on a video maker in California who had nothing to do with the assault.

Now we know from what you just read why the Obama administration did so much harm to this nation. He moved the country in unprecedented levels of debt—about $6.5 trillion in five years. He called his predecessor "unpatriotic" for adding $5 trillion debt in eight years. He has fashioned a country in which more people now receive government aid, means tested—let alone nonmeans tested—than work full-time. Obama is equally true domestically and internationally. Domestically, his policies have gravely impacted the American economy. He has overseen the weakest recovery from a recession in modern American history. The only question is whether this can ever be undone.

At first, who cared whether Iran serially violated every Obama deadline on halting nuclear enrichment? Did we worry that Libya, where Obama led from behind, was descending into Somalia? Few Americans were all that bothered over Obama's empty order to Syrian president Bashar Assad to step down or over Obama's later various redline threats that bombs would follow a use of chemical weapons by Assad.

The man Obama fears the most is Sean Hannity on Fox News cable show. To say that Obama hates Fox News may be an understatement. Obama said in one of his speeches that if he listened to Fox News, "I would not vote for myself." Robert Ailes, president of Fox News, America's number one rated cable news channel, doesn't mince words. He said that Obama lied to him at their first meeting, which took place in 2008 at New York's Waldorf Astoria Hotel with News Corporation chairman and CEO Rupert Murdock in the room. When Ailes confronted Obama about his plan for unilateral arms cuts, Obama denied he ever made such a statement. It was as good a lie as anyone ever told.

Barack Obama and Communism

Art Moore has written some interesting information about Obama's background and how he has been influenced by his communist friends. "Never in the history of the United States of America has a president had a mentor (Frank Marshall Davis) who is a literal card-carrying member of the Communist Party." If you want to hear Davis in Obama rhetoric and ideas, you can begin with Obama's vow on the eve of his historic election to bring "fundamental change" to the United States, the exact term Davis used to describe Communism. Paul Kengor, an author and political science professor at Grove City College, pointed out that when Davis launched the communist *Chicago Star* newspaper in 1946, he called for a "new Declaration of Independence" in his first column. Davis wrote that history teachers alluding to the Marxist dialectic that "any fundamental change advancing society is spearheaded by strong radicals." Kengor noted Obama never once give his full name in his book *Dreams from My Father*, a clear indication that he knows how radical Frank Davis was. Davis' communist activities in Chicago put him on the radar of the FBI and Congress in the 1940s and 1950s before he moved to Hawaii in the 1960s and began to frequently receive Obama in his Honolulu home in the 1970s. Obama uses Frank's name twenty-two times in *Dreams* and refers to him with pronouns in many other instances and describes him in his autobiography as a father figure, with a permanent influence on his life, whose counsel helped him navigate his teen years and guide him into his adulthood.

In his research for *The Communist*, Kengor combed through declassified FBI files and visited archives and Davis's original newspaper columns to document the black Communist Party activists' support of Mao's China and Stalin's USSR. He shows how Davis's ideas have turned up in Obama's policies, including wealth distribution, government stimulus for "public works projects," and taxpayer funding of universal health care and nationalizing General Motors. Kengor thinks the relationship with Davis might be behind Obama's decision to send the bust of Winston Churchill back to Britain. This was given to the United States as a gift after the September 11 attacks on the World Trade Center. "I mean Churchill is America's man of the century, let alone Britain's man of the century, then I found out that Frank Marshall Davis despised Churchill," said Kengor. Despite Davis's prominent role in Obama's life, liberals in general and even many conservatives have ignored him or obscured or downplayed his Communist Party activism. Kengor said, "For liberals, there is nothing that seems to anger them more than anti-Communist." He continued, "It is not that liberals are pro-Communist, even though liberals do share certain sympathies with Communists on certain things, but liberals absolutely detest anti-Communists. So any conservative who comes along and raises the specter of Obama's communist past or his past associations, liberals just come at him full force, with howitzers, hand grenades—everything—all cannons firing." Kengor found a remarkable lineage between the Chicago political family in which Davis rose in the 1940s and the Chicago political family in the White House of Obama. Obama described his most trusted aide, Valerie Jarrett, "like a sibling to me." She is the daughter-in-law of Vernon Jarrett who worked as a communist activist with Davis in the 1940s. David Cantor's father, Harry Jacob Carter, was the secretary of the Boston Communist Party. David Axelrod's mother worked for a magazine known for its communist leanings.

Kengor says Obama is clearly "on the far left," and there is strong evidence he was a Communist when he was a student at Occidental. "I could easily in a court of law prove that Frank Marshall Davis was a Communist. But when it comes to explaining Obama, the establishment media has shown virtually no interest in delving into the life of the man the president himself held up as a guiding and affirming voice at every major point in Barrack Obama's life," said Paul Kengor.

Race Relations

The Trump administration will do a much-better job of race relations. President Trump made the first good move by appointing Dr. Ben Carson to his cabinet. They will work together by going into the poor inner-city neighborhoods and building better housing and better-paying jobs for all minority commuter workers. They should make sure teenagers have an opportunity to find work. They should make sure that men and women of all races have an equal opportunity for job openings. When you have people with good jobs and good wages, you don't have protests and riots in the streets. President Trump has made it a priority to help all minorities, and he will keep his promise like all other campaign promises.

Watching President Trump interact with various races of people, he seems to be comfortable and at ease with conservatives than with liberals. In many of his speeches, President Trump makes it clear that liberal politicians and their policies did not make this country great. He and all of us know that the founders of this country were conservative and they wrote a conservative Constitution. I believe most of us agree that conservatives then and now make our country great. That is also why so many immigrants want to become US citizens.

The Muslim Culture

President Trump says Muslims are the ones causing problems all over the world. He then gives many different reasons how this causes problems throughout the world. There are specific things Obama said that President Trump disagrees with, that is:

   a. Obama said America is not a Christian nation.
   b. He spoke these words at an Islamic dinner: "I am one of you."
   c. On ABC News, he referenced "my Muslim faith."
   d. He sat for twenty years in a Liberation Theology Church that condemns Christianity and professes Marxism.
   e. Obama purposefully omitted "endowed by our creator" from recitation of the Declaration of Independence.
   f. He mocked the Bible of Jesus Christ's Sermon on the Mount while repeatedly referring to the holy Koran.
   g. Obama traveled the Islamic world denigrating the United States.
   h. He refused to attend the National Prayer Breakfast but hastened to host an Islamic prayer breakfast at the White House.
   i. He ordered Georgetown University and Notre Dame University to shroud all vestiges of Jesus Christ before he would agree to speak there. In contrast, he never requested that mosques he visited to adjust their decor.
   j. Obama gave $100 million in US taxpayer funds to rebuild foreign mosques.
   k. He curtailed the military tribunals of all Islamic terrorists.

l. He was the first president not to give a Christmas greeting from the White House and went so far as to hang photographs of Chairman Mao on the Christmas tree.
m. Obama said that NASA's "foremost mission" was an outreach to Muslim communities. He wrote that in the event of a conflict, "I will stand with the Muslims."
n. Obama appointed radical Islamists to Homeland Security, and he appointed anti-Christian fanatics to his Czar Corps.
o. He exempted Muslims from penalties under Obamacare that the rest of the people must pay.
p. Obama assured the Egyptian Foreign Minister that "I am a Muslin," and he bowed in submission before the Saudi Arabia king.
q. He did not go to France to show solidarity against the Muslim terrorists.
r. Obama appointed Valerie Jarrett, an Iranian, as his chief adviser. She is a member of the Muslim Sisterhood, which is an offshoot of the Muslim Brotherhood.
s. Obama was uncharacteristically quick to join the chorus of the Muslim Brotherhood to depose Egypt's Hosni Mubarak, formerly America's strongest ally in North Africa, but he remained muted in his nonresponse to the brotherhood-led slaughter of Egyptian Christians.
t. Obama refused to condemn the Fort Hood killer as an Islamic terrorist.
u. He and his family departed for Hawaii over the Christmas season to avoid past criticism for not participating in seasonal White House religious events.
v. He refused to speak out concerning the horrific executions of women throughout the Muslim culture but submitted Arizona to the United Nations for investigation of hypothetical human rights abuses.
w. He funneled $900 million in US taxpayer dollars to Hamas.
x. He ordered the US Postal Service to honor the Muslim holiday with a new commemorative stamp.

y.   He funneled mandatory Arabic language and culture studies in grammar schools across our country.
z.   He followed the Muslim custom of not wearing any form of jewelry during Ramadan.

When you compare what Obama says to what President Trump says as a Christian believer, be thankful that the president will lead the United States with Christian values, not Muslim values.

President Trump has a good man in his cabinet, Ben Carson, who has a great deal of knowledge about Muslims. Dr. Carson was asked the question, Can Muslims be good Americans? Listed below are some of the reasons he said Muslims cannot be good Americans:

- Religiously no, because no other religion is accepted by his Allah except Islam.
- Scripturally no, because his allegiance is to the five pillars of Islam and the Koran.
- Geographically no, because his allegiance is to Mecca, to which he turns in prayer five times a day.
- Socially no, because his allegiance to Islam forbids him from making friends with Christians or Jews.
- Politically no, because he must submit to the mullahs (spiritual leaders) who teach annihilation of Israel and destruction of America, the "Great Satan."
- Domestically no, because he is instructed to marry four women and beat and scourge a wife when she disobeys him.
- Intellectually no, because he cannot accept the American constitution since it is based on biblical principles and he believes the Bible to be corrupt.
- Philosophically no, because Islam, Muhammad, and the Koran do not allow freedom of religion and expression. Democracy and Islam cannot coexist. Every Muslim government is dictatorial or autocratic.
- Spiritually no, because when we declare "one nation under God," the Christian God is loving and kind, while Allah is

never referred to as heavenly Father, nor is he ever called love in the Koran's ninety-nine excellent names.

Therefore, after much study and deliberation, perhaps we should be very suspicious of Muslims in this country. They obviously cannot be both "good" Muslins and "good" Americans. Call it what you wish; it's still the truth and you had better believe it. The more people who understand this, the better it will be for our country and our future. The religious war is bigger than we know or understand. The Muslims have said they will destroy us from within. So freedom is not free.

For those who care about the future, read what Nonie Darwish has said. In the Muslim faith, a Muslim man can marry a child as young as one-year-old and have sexual intimacy with this child, consummating the marriage by age nine. The dowry is given to the family of the groom in exchange for the woman (who becomes his slave) and for the purchase of her private parts to use her as a toy. In the Western world (America), Muslim men are starting to demand Sharia law so the wife cannot obtain a divorce and he can have complete control over her. It is amazing and alarming how many of our sisters and daughters attending American universities are now marrying Muslim men and submitting themselves and their children to Sharia law. Nonie says radical Islamists are working to impose Sharia on the world. If that happens, Western civilization will be destroyed. In twenty years, there will be enough Muslim voters in the United States to elect the president by themselves! Rest assured they will do so. You can look at how they have taken over several towns in the United States. Dearborn, Michigan, is one, and there are others. This is information about Muslims that most Americans do not know. We must wake up and realize what the Muslims are doing in our country.

Mr. Obama refused to speak out concerning the horrific executions of women throughout the Muslim culture, but he submitted Arizona to the United Nations for investigation of hypothetical human rights abuses. Obama funded mandatory Arabic language and culture studies in grammar schools across our country. Obama follows the Muslim custom of not wearing any form of jewelry during Ramadan. When queried in India, he refused to acknowledge the true extent of radical global jihadists and instead profusely praised Islam in a country that is 82 percent Hindu and the victim of numerous Islamic terrorist assaults. Obama furnished $900 million in US taxpayer dollars to Hamas. Obama directed our United Kingdom embassy to conduct outreach to help "empower" the British Muslims community. Obama ordered the US Postal Service to honor the Muslim holiday with a new commemorative stamp.

President Trump's administration asks if there is a third US political party. How about the Muslin Brotherhood? The radical Muslim Brotherhood has built the framework for a political party in America that seeks to turn Muslims into an Islamist voting bloc. Muslim voters have the potential to be swing voters in American elections. The Muslim Brotherhood's recently exposed goal is to wage a "civilization jihad" against America that explicitly calls for infiltrating the US political system and destroying it from within, also establish Sharia law. What we must realize is who the Muslims are.

Here are a few examples of their actions: The Israeli Olympic team attackers were Muslims. The London subway bombers were Muslims. The shoe bomber was a Muslim. The Fort Hood shooter was a Muslim. The USS Cole bomber was a Muslim. The underwear bomber was a Muslim. The Boston marathon bombers were Muslims. The Pan American Flight 93 bombers were Muslims. The Beirut marine barracks bombers were Muslims. So what are the major terrorist organizations? They are Islamic Jihad, ISIS, al-Qaeda, Taliban, Hamas, Hezbollah, Boko Haram, al-Nusra, Abu Sayyaf, al-Bakr, and Muslim Brotherhood. With this information, it is easy to figure out who's causing the problems.

A friend was in a neighborhood grocery store checkout line. She was wearing a necklace with a Christian cross around her neck. The woman checking her out was a woman dressed as a Muslim. She asked her to take it off as it offended her. She declined the request. So she called over her Muslim supervisor, and he asked my friend to take off the necklace because it offended the cashier. My friend said she would not take it off and left her groceries on the counter and walked out. The man behind her witnessed the whole thing, and he also left his groceries and walked out.

Disloyal Holdovers

President Trump said once upon a time, the United States was the most loved and most respected nation on this planet, but those days are gone. We have wrecked out economy, lost our values, and fumbled away our future. But if you look closely enough, you can still see some of the things that once made this nation a shining beacon to the rest of the world. This includes some weird facts but also some very troubling facts. For example, if we are ever going to change the course as a nation, we need to come to grips with how far we have fallen. When a president occasionally fails to tell the truth, you get a scandal like the monitoring of Associated Press reports. When a president serially fails to tell the truth, you get that plus the scandals involving the IRS, the NSR, the Veterans Administration, Benghazi, and too many others to mention. But I must mention this one—in the first two months of President Trump's time in office, the IRS leaked to the news media his 2005 income tax information. By law, this is a felony crime, which means that the person who did this can go to jail.

Leaks are some of the most troubling things that are happening to the Trump administration. One of the main reasons this is happening is because so many Obama administration people still have their jobs. There is good reason to believe that Obama holdovers are disloyal to Mr. Trump. Some of these Obama holdovers are part of the shadow government that Obama has put in place to leak information that will hurt Mr. Trump. We all know how the WikiLeaks haunted the Clinton campaign.

Abortion/Pro-Life

Democrats say, "Trust the woman to make personal and responsible decisions regarding when or whether to bear children, in consultation with their family, their physician, their personal conscious, or their God, rather than having these personal decisions made by politicians. Recognize that the product of a joined egg and sperm has no independent status, standing, entitlements, or rights that would usurp or supersede in any way the rights, status, standing, and decisions of the mother or woman, which are paramount." Democrats plainly say when it comes to abortion, they are proabortion. Republicans say, about life, all innocent human life must be respected and safeguarded from fertilization to natural death; therefore, the unborn child, the aged, and the physically or mentally challenged have a fundamental individual right to life, which cannot be infringed upon. Republicans plainly say when it comes to abortion, they are *pro-life*.

Gun Control

President Trump has very strong views about gun control. He believes the American founding fathers wrote the second amendment with clear intent—no level of government shall regulate either the ownership or possession of firearms.

Therefore, he strongly opposes all laws that infringe on the right to bear arms. He opposes the monitoring of gun ownership and the taxation and regulation of guns, ammunition, and gun magazines. Trump collectively urged the legislature to pass constitutional carry legislation whereby law-abiding citizens who possess firearms can legally exercise the God-given right to carry that firearm as well. Until each time, we urge the reintroduction and pass legislation easing current restrictions on firearms such as open carry and campus carry. What President Trump is saying is all people love the right of protecting themselves and their family. This is a God-given right at this time in our history because of the evil crime rate that has been going up the last few years. During his presidential campaign, Mr. Trump mentioned Chicago's crime rate as an example of what is happening in many of our cities. One of his campaign promises was to bring down crimes in inner cities. Drug use is one of the main causes of crime in the United States. Trump opposes legalization of illicit and synthetic drugs. He supports an effective abstinence based on educational programs for children. He opposes any needle exchange program. Trump urges vigorous enforcement of all drug laws. He believes crime and terrorism are major threats to international peace and to our safety.

Economy/Jobs

The economy of this country is in very bad shape. President Trump and his administration have put forth the changes that will bring back the economy to its greatness. One of the ways the economy will improve is to add new jobs. The many regulations the Obama administration placed on businesses made it difficult to start and grow a business. Lower taxes will help businesses to have the money to grow and employ more people. Energy independence will help individuals and businesses to have the freedom to spend money and stimulate the economy. Reworked Obamacare will cost less money and will put more money into everyone's pocket, which will stimulate the economy. Bringing back businesses and manufacturers from overseas will certainly create jobs and money for this country. The reason it is so important for this money to come back to the United States is we will have the money to rebuild our great military, roads and railroads, as well as the other infrastructure that is in need of repairs and replacement.

The Trump administration has indicated the ten most important things it must accomplish at the beginning of the first term in office. One is to bring back businesses and jobs that have moved to foreign countries. A recent survey discovered that "a steady job" is the number one thing that American women are looking for in a husband and that 75 percent of women would have a serious problem dating an unemployed man. Also, according to a study conducted by economists, up to 47 percent of the jobs in the United States could soon be lost to computers, robots, and other forms of technology. This administration has done a great deal to create jobs in its first two months in office. In the month of January, 350,000 jobs were created. This is one hundred thousand more than was expected. Many of these new jobs are well paying. President Trump has been working with business CEOs to move these manufacturing plants from foreign countries back to the United States. This move back to the United States was taking place even before he took office. President Trump has been meeting with labor unions and blue-collar worker organizations regularly since taking office. This administration has given the go-ahead to start working on jobs that Obama had put on hold. The oil pipeline from Canada to Texas is now being completed. With his strict government regulations, Obama had shut down many jobs that would have been working.

In his agenda to create jobs, President Trump will have all kinds of infrastructure jobs, that is, repair old and build new bridges and repaid old and build new highways, new tunnels, and new railroads, to name a few. A few of the infrastructure jobs are shovel ready. President Trump is keeping his promise to provide jobs for blue-collar workers. In a short time, he has created jobs for all people who want to work. This proved that the president has great respect and love for ordinary citizens. He has shown this respect and love at political rallies. This is the reason so many people turn out for his rallies.

These people are very loyal to the president. They get up before sunrise to attend his rallies. They sometimes stand in line for five to six hours to be sure they get in where he is speaking. This kind of response to Mr. Trump is because of the simple, straightforward way he speaks to people. If he keeps his campaign promises, he will continue to talk directly to the people and the fraud media, and the establishment politicians can't keep him from being an eight-year president. Many people are conservative and will always turn out for his rallies and turn out to vote for him.

President Trump has the background and the agenda plans to create jobs. His plans to create jobs were one of his campaign promises that he talked about most. Like all his promises, he has lived up to this promise. In fact, before he was sworn into office, he caused companies that were going to move their business operation to foreign countries to remain in this country to grow and create jobs for the American worker. President Trump has been very successful since he has been in office to cause many companies that have factories in foreign countries to move those factories back to the United Sates; this creates jobs. President Trump by executive order has given many business tax breaks that helped many companies to survive. Also, the new tax regulations helped new companies to start up and be successful. As long as Mr. Trump is our president, you can count on him to help new companies of all kinds start up and grow. A good thing will happen because of all these new jobs—it will stop a lot of marches and protests from happening because these people will have jobs. President Trump has very strong feelings about improving the racial problems this country has with the different nationalities and cultures.

The Trump administration says, "We oppose government regulation (the Employment Non-Discrimination Act), which would coerce business owners and employees to violate their own conscious, beliefs, and principles." Democrats strongly oppose discrimination or harassment in any institution of higher education against any person based on race, sex, color, religion, national origin, ancestry, age, mental status, disability, sexual orientation, gender identity, expression, or military status. The differences between Republicans and Democrats are very clear regarding how they feel about discrimination. Republicans give you the freedom of choice. Democrats very specifically tell you who you can or cannot discriminate against.

President Trump is for states to have government control and help their people to be successful. The federal government's most important job is to keep this country safe and support state governments. President Trump is very qualified to do this with his successful background in the business world. His top agenda promise is to create jobs and build a strong economy. Most of the people in this country believe President Trump's agenda is the right agenda. When you think about what the current administration is doing and will continue to do, it is hard to understand why the liberals and news media cannot see how the Trump agenda is helping in many ways to make this country great again.

Immigration

One of Mr. Trump's campaign promises was to remove illegal immigrants who have committed crimes. People know what illegal immigrants are doing in this country. We read newspapers, listen to radio, and view television and learn what is happening. I read the *Dallas Morning News* from front to back. Most every day, I read about criminal acts by illegal immigrants. I believe, like President Trump, every one of these people should be rounded up and deported to their country of origin. Legal immigration has been a good thing for the most part. President Trump says people who come to this country and do not learn the language and laws do not love this country and need to go home. They are here just to take advantage of all the benefits this country offers. They want to live here in ways that reflect the culture of their home country. President Trump has said in many ways that immigrants in the United States should not protest and mock us with the flag of their country of origin.

 One of the most pressing problems is what to do about immigration. The Obama administration refused to enforce federal law on illegal aliens. The propaganda fraud media has put out so much bad information about immigration; it is hard to know what to believe. We all want legal immigration, but we are opposed to illegal immigration. President Trump has done a good job of keeping us informed about illegals coming into this country. Per one report, in 2017, nearly 20,000 illegal immigrants committed roughly 64,000 crimes, including 12,307 drunken-driving convictions, 1,728 cases of assault, 216 kidnappings, and more than 200 homicide or manslaughter convictions. Entering this country illegally is breaking the law. They should realize that to become a citizen of this country, they must pay the price. President Trump has made it clear that he is a "law and order" president.

President Trump believes in legal immigration like most people of the United States. He realizes what can happen if immigrants continue to move into this country, how the culture will change, and our way of government could change. This change could happen sooner than we think if the Muslim population continues to gain strength in state and federal government until they are in control. Americans need to stop and think about what happened in Germany in the 1920s and 1930s.

Very few people in Germany were true Nazis. But many people enjoyed the return of German pride, and many more were too busy to care. Most people thought the Nazis were a bunch of fools. So the majority sat back and let the Nazis take control of the German government. When people sit back and do nothing, the aggressive and organized people take over control of the government of that nation. President Trump understands how this happened in other countries and is making sure that the United States does not let that happen here. The way President Trump is changing our immigration laws is a good start in the right direction.

President Trump's executive order changed the way people come into the United States. They are very closely checked out and vetted before they are allowed to enter this country. The various ways you can enter the United States are, as a tourist, with a visa for a period of time and when immigrants come here to become a new citizen. President Trump has been very open and straightforward with an executive order to arrest every illegal immigrant criminal and return them to their home country. If they try to come back, they are caught and arrested again, and they will be charged with a felony arrest and go to prison. Most people of this country support what the president is doing about stricter control of immigrants entering the United States and building of the southern border wall.

Immigrants have come to this country for all the wrong reasons, namely:

1. Receive free medical care
2. Receive free food stamps

3. Receive free housing
4. Speak their own language and not learn English
5. Not learn the American culture
6. Not pay taxes or Social Security
7. Earn money and send back to their home country
8. Have children who will be born American citizens
9. Bring in all kinds of illegal drugs
10. Commit robberies and other crimes

President Trump has made it very clear that he will build the wall and stop it from being so easy to enter this country illegally. In the first few months of President Trump's tenure, southern border crossings are down 40 percent. Don't forget that Congress passed a bill for a secure fence in 2006 but never fully funded it. For all the hysteria about "Trump's wall," more than two dozen Senate Democrats voted for the Secure Fence Act, including Senate Democrat leader Charles Schumer (D-NY), as well as then senators Barack Obama, Joe Biden, and Hillary Clinton. The Trump administration has made it clear that they will be strictly vetting all people who come into the United States, from some countries more than others. People from some radical Muslim countries will not be let in for a period of time. President Trump is determined to keep radical Muslims out of our country. He knows what is happening in many countries (protests and riots) such as in France, Germany, England, and other countries. Think of people who have been killed by radical Muslims. Some of these radicals have been deported from our country five or more times.

President Trump's agenda to build the wall on our southern border is in the works already. Contractors are submitting bids, and the Trump administration is looking for ways to finance it. The president has given us good reasons to build the wall. One reason is to stop drugs from coming into the United States and to stop all kinds of weapons from going into Mexico. But the big problem is to stop illegal immigrants from crossing our southern border. Most all our communities have been affected by loss of jobs and low wages; the economy affected by taxes not paid, unsafe neighborhoods, and schools underperforming. President Trump supports and encourages legal immigration. He thinks enforcing existing laws will go a long way in stopping illegal immigration.

To make it personal, how would you feel if a radical Muslim killed your mother or father, brother or sister? Partisan news networks such as CNN and MSNBC soft sell this kind of news, so why watch their networks? You do not get the truth when you watch CNN and MSNBC.

Here's another idea: tax the remittance (money) sent to Mexico by immigrants in this country. It has been estimated that Mexico received more than $20 billion in remittances last year (2016). The vast majority of it was sent by illegal immigrants.

As a World War II veteran, I resent anyone marching and displaying a foreign flag at their home or business or attached to their car. Veterans have a special love for this country and resent the flag being insulted in any way. The flag of the United States should always be honored and respected. I do not feel that veterans are special or more important than anyone else, but we are very patriotic.

Many illegal immigrants deal in illegal drugs, commit robbery, have traffic violations, and get free health care and free food stamps. President Trump says these people will be arrested and sent back to their home country. They will be arrested and charged with a felony. President Trump has his own strategy and policies to deal with illegal immigration and how to make America safe and better again. He is not afraid to make hard and difficult decisions; he always wants to do the right thing. He knows what he is doing and why he is doing it. Immigrants caught with fake documents or IDs will be charged with aggravated identity theft. This new government approach to illegal immigration makes us feel at ease and safe at home, at work, and on our streets and highways.

With Trump's information, most of the facts and statistics were taken from the *Denver Post* newspaper. Over 80 percent of Americans demand secured borders and illegal migration stopped. But what would happen if all twenty million or more illegals vacated America? In California, if 3.5 million illegal aliens moved back to Mexico, it would leave an extra $10.2 billion to spend on an overloaded school system, bankrupt hospitals, and overrun prisons. It would leave highways cleaner, safer, and less congested. Everyone could understand one another as English would become the dominant language again.

In Colorado, five hundred thousand illegal migrants, plus their three hundred thousand kids and grandchildren, would move back "home" mostly to Mexico. That would save Colorado an estimated $2 billion (other experts say $7 billion) annually in taxes that pay for schooling, medical, social services, and incarceration costs. It means twelve thousand gang members would vanish out of Denver alone. Colorado would save more than $20 million in prison costs, and the terror that 7,300 alien criminals set upon citizens would be gone. Denver police officer Don Young and hundreds of Colorado victims would not have suffered death, accidents, rapes, and other crimes by illegals. Denver public schools would not suffer a 67 percent dropout and failure rate because of thousands of illegal alien students speaking forty-one different languages. At least two hundred thousand vehicles would vanish from our gridlocked cities in Colorado. Denver's 4 percent unemployment rate would vanish as our working poor would gain jobs at a living wage.

In Florida, 1.5 million illegals would return the Sunshine State back to America, the rule of law and English. In Chicago, Illinois, 2.1 million illegals would free up hospitals, schools, prisons, and highways for a safer, cleaner, and more crime-free experience.

If twenty million illegal aliens returned home, the US economy would return to the rule of law. Employers would hire legal American citizens at a living wage. Everyone would pay their fair share of taxes because they wouldn't be working off the books. That would result in an additional $401 billion in IRS income taxes collected annually and an equal amount for local, state, and city coffers. No more "press 1 for English" or "press 2 for Spanish." No more confusion in American schools that now must contend with over one hundred languages that degrade the educational systems for American kids. Our overcrowded schools would lose more than two million illegal alien kids at a cost of billions in ESL and free breakfast and lunches. We would lose five hundred thousand illegal criminal alien inmates at a cost of more than $1.6 billion annually. That includes fifteen thousand MS-13 gang members who distribute $130 billion in drugs annually who would vacate our country.

In cities like Los Angeles, twenty thousand members of the Eighteenth Street Gang would vanish from our nation. No more Mexican forgery gangs for identification theft from Americans. No more foreign rapists and child molesters! Losing more than twenty thousand million people would clear up our crowded highways and gridlock. Cleaner air and less drinking and driving American deaths by illegal aliens! American economy is drained; taxpayers are taxed. Employers get rich.

Over $80 billion annually wouldn't return to the aliens' home countries by cash transfers. Illegal migrants earned half that amount of untaxed money that further drained American economy, which currently suffers a *$20 trillion debt*! At least four hundred thousand anchor babies would not be born in our country, costing us $109 billion per year per cycle.

At least eighty-six hospitals in California, Florida, and Georgia would still be operating instead of being bankrupt and out of existence because illegals pay nothing via the EMTALA Act. Americans would not suffer thousands of TB and hepatitis cases rampant in our country brought in by illegals crossing our borders. Twenty million fewer people would be driving, polluting, and gridlocking our cities and would also put the "progressives" on the horns of a dilemma. Illegal aliens and their families cause 11 percent of our greenhouse gases.

Over one million of Mexico's poorest citizens now live inside and along our border from Brownsville, Texas, to San Diego, California, in what the *New York Times* "colonies" or new neighborhoods. Those living areas resemble Bombay and Calcutta where grinding poverty, filth, diseases, drugs, crimes, and no sanitation exist. They live without sewage, clean water, paved streets and roads, electricity, and no proper sanitation. The *New York Times* reported them to be America's new "third world" inside our own country. At the current rate of growth, in twenty years they expect twenty million residents in those colonies. Many people who have personally seen this in Texas and Arizona say it is sickening and beyond anything you can imagine.

By enforcing our laws, we could repatriate them to Mexico. We should invite twenty million aliens to go home, fix their own country, and/or make a better life in Mexico. We already invite a million people into our country annually, more than all other countries combined. We cannot and must not allow anarchy at our borders, more within our borders, and growing lawlessness at every level in our nation. It's time to stand up for our country, our culture, our civilization, and our way of life.

Here are thirteen reasons illegal aliens should vacate America:

1. Each year, $14 billion to $22 billion is spent on welfare for illegal aliens. (That's billion with a "B"!)
2. Each year, $7.5 billion are spent on Medicaid for illegal aliens.
3. Each year, $12 billion are spent on primary and secondary school education for illegal children, and they still can't speak a word of English.
4. Each year, $27 million is spent to educate American-born children of illegals, known as "anchor babies."
5. To incarcerate illegal aliens, $3 million per day is spent. That is $1.2 billion a year.
6. A total of twenty-eight percent of all federal prison inmates are illegal aliens.
7. A total of $190 billion per year in suppressed American wages is caused by illegal aliens for welfare and social services by the American taxpayers.
8. A total of $200 billion per year in suppressed American wages is caused by illegal aliens.
9. Illegal aliens in the United States have a crime rate two and a half times that of white nonillegal aliens. Their children are going to make a huge additional crime problem in the United States.
10. During the year 2005, there were 8 to 10 million illegal aliens that crossed our southern border with as many as 19,500 illegals from other terrorist countries. Over 10,000

of those were Middle-Eastern terrorists. Millions of pounds of drugs (cocaine, meth, heroin, crack, and marijuana) plus guns crossed into the United States from the southern border.
11. The National Policy Institute estimates that the total cost of mass deportation would be between $206 and $230 billion, or an average cost of between $41 and $46 billion annually over a five-year period.
12. In 2006, illegal aliens sent home $65 billion in remittances to their families and friends back in their countries of origin.
13. On the dark side of illegal immigration, nearly one million sex crimes are committed in the United States. The total cost is a whopping $38.3 billion a year. Use your common sense and think about this information. You can then understand why President Trump is so strong for a southern border wall and extreme vetting of everyone who comes into this country. Everyone agrees on legal immigration because we are a loving, caring people who want to help those in need. But sometimes, we must make the hard decision that we put Americans first.

Two of President Trump's campaign promises were to keep us informed and to keep America first and safe. He accomplished these two promises with the new immigration laws. I've said this earlier, but it is so important that I want to say it again—President Trump thinks, talks, and acts like the people of the World War II generation. The greatest assets of that generation are they were honest; they had good common sense and accepted personal responsibility for who they claimed to be. If Donald Trump had entered the race to become president of the United States in the 1930s and 1940s during WWII, he would have won his first four-year term and a second four-year term in a landslide.

President Trump has made it very clear that the United States will no longer stand down and let aggressive countries commit their atrocities against another nation. This was the attitude of the WWII generation. President Trump will keep these attitudes and beliefs as long as he is our president. One of President Trump's promises was to be transparent and keep us informed about foreign relations with other nations. He will not do like the Obama administration did and tell foreign leaders in advance what action he planned against them. President Trump said he will always keep his word about what action he plans to take. The president and his advisers will keep all planned actions against other nations secret until he is ready to proceed. Totalitarian, aggressive nations that are bullies and tyrants only respect toughness and strength, like Germany and Japan before WWII. There is just one answer to nations that take this approach to their foreign policy—"defeat and destroy them."

The Story about Old White Men

This is the story about old white men: they founded the thirteen colonies of this country; they organized the first government—a democracy of free people. Old white men were mainly the ones who took up arms and won independence from England; they are the people who wrote the Constitution and the Bill of Rights. More than any other group since the founding of this country, they have been the presidents, governors, congressmen, mayors, and city councilmen. Do you understand what I am saying? To keep it true and simple, old white men have been the backbone of this country from its beginning. This is said to the liberals who complain and do very little for this country, and the old white man does everything that's good about the United States. Like President Trump's team that he has organized to run this country, they are qualified, experienced, successful, and mostly men who know how to plan, organize, and do the job that needs to be done.

Conclusion

The president realizes he is hampered by the left-wing infighting of his party. With his confidence and ability to influence control and deal with people, he knows he can work out a solution to this problem because of his background experiences. It is his way to reboot and make his decisions. He knows that when the dust settles, he wins. This is the attitude and character of a presidential leader. Also, this is a president who is not easily convinced he is wrong about most any decision. The reason President Trump can get by with this management style is because he managed his businesses and now manages the country as president. He puts high value on loyalty for his team. His team values loyalty as well. They are men and women with experience and are qualified with a successful background in their chosen fields. President Trump is to be congratulated for getting together such a great team to lead the country and make it great again. Mr. Trump is the very definition of the American success story, continually setting the standards of excellence in business, real estate, entertainment, and now politics. He is a dealmaker without peer.

With the Obama administration, it was smoke and mirrors; and at the White House, the buck stopped nowhere. After reading all this information, you can see why President Trump said he inherited a mess. Obama handed President Trump a basketful of hand grenades with the pins pulled. It is very difficult to listen to the harsh, ugly talk of the liberals when you know that the reality and final answer is they are wrong and will lose to the conservatives because the conservatives have the correct agenda and policies.

In closing, I have one more opinion. It is beyond my understanding how people who disagree with President Trump can be so crude, cruel, and vicious with hate toward him. President Trump is a Christian and does not hate anyone. (I am a Christian and I do not hate anyone.) I hope this book encourages every voter to be knowledgeable and fair-minded about President Trump. His agenda is what this country needs to make America great again. President Trump loves this country, and he loves all the people in the United States.

Now I will be a prophet and make a few predictions. The liberal Democrats don't seem to have an open mind or common sense to learn the truth. They shout and rant about how they are going to destroy and defeat President Trump. They said there was no way Hillary could lose the election to Trump. Liberals first went on and on about how Hillary would beat Trump. Now they are claiming that the Democrats will win in the 2018 election year. I predict President Trump and the Republicans will win and add seats in the United States House and Senate in 2018. Republicans will win most of the elections in states and counties and local elections. President Trump will appoint two more conservative Supreme Court Justices. President Trump's people running for elected offices will continue to win, win, win. The liberal activists/demonstrators who are doing so much to hurt and damage this country will lose, lose, lose. Present-day liberal leadership will not regain power for the Democrats. They are not talented, experienced, or qualified leaders that impress and win voters to the Democratic Party. Liberal fake media hurt the Democratic Party, and they are so partisan to the point of being disloyal to the United States. Honest TV networks have given out information that proved this to be true.

Survey of World War II Veterans (44) What Do You Think about What Is Happening in the United States?

1. Is the United States going in the right direction?   Yes   <u>8</u>   No   <u>35</u>

2. Do you think Barack Obama is doing a good job as president?   Yes   <u>4</u>   No   <u>40</u>

3. Do you believe in more or less government control?   More   <u>0</u>   Less   <u>44</u>

4. You are eighteen years old again, would you volunteer to serve in a war now?   Yes   <u>18</u>   No   <u>25</u>

5. Are you a conservative or a liberal?   Con.   <u>41</u>   Lib.   <u>3</u>

6. Are you a Republican or Democrat or "Other"?   Rep.   <u>36</u>   Dem.   <u>4</u>   Other   <u>2</u>

7. Do you approve of waterboarding the enemy to get information?   Yes   <u>33</u>   No   <u>10</u>

8. Do you think we should close Guantanamo (Gitmo) Prison?   Yes   <u>10</u>   No   <u>32</u>

9. Did you vote for Obama or Romney?   Obam   <u>4</u>   Rom   <u>38</u>

10. Do you think Obama is honest and straightforward when delivering his political speeches?	Yes	5	No	37				
11. Is Obama or Congress more at fault for the condition this country is in?	Obam	28	Con	17				
12. Do you believe in free enterprise or Socialism?	Free	44	Soc	0				
13. Do you believe openly gay men and women should serve in the military?	Yes	8	No	34				
14. Should women serve on the front line in combat?	Yes	4	No	39				
15. Does Obama take too many vacations?	Yes	36	No	8				
16. Does Obama spend too much money on parties/entertainment?	Yes	38	No	5				
17. Do you think too many people are on food stamps?	Yes	39	No	4				
18. Do you believe in same-sex marriage?	Yes	4	No	39				
19. Is there too much partisanship in Washington, DC?	Yes	33	No	9				
20. Is national debt or lack of jobs the government's biggest problem?	Debt	29	Jobs	15				
21. Has racism under Obama become worse?	Yes	34	No	7				
22. Which is this country's biggest problem?	N. Korea	10	Iran	12	Afghanistan	13		

THE HONEST TRUTH ABOUT DONALD TRUMP

23. Should we bomb nuclear bomb factories in Iran and N. Korea?	Yes	<u>23</u>	No	<u>21</u>
24. Should we give more support to Israel?	Yes	<u>35</u>	No	<u>9</u>
25. Do you believe in government loans for college students?	Yes	<u>39</u>	No	<u>5</u>
26. Should students go to jail if they do not repay government loans?	Yes	<u>28</u>	No	<u>13</u>
27. Do you think the government should *give poor people fish or teach them to fish (work)*?	Give	<u>0</u>	Teach	<u>44</u>
28. Do you believe in a one-party or two-party system of government?	One	<u>0</u>	Two	<u>44</u>
29. Do you think the national media is fair and balanced to both Democrats and Republicans? Who is the most fair and balanced news person? Name: Greta, 2; Lear, Hannity, Brower, Brian Williams, and Krauthammer, 2; O'Reilly, 3	Yes	<u>2</u>	No	<u>31</u>
30. Are there too many unqualified and inexperienced people in government jobs?	<u>Yes</u>	<u>44</u>	No	<u>0</u>
31. Do you think Obama has taken a strong-enough stance against terrorists?	Yes	<u>7</u>	No	<u>33</u>

32. The Obama administration is very "transparent." Yes 2   No   37

33. People are very careful about what they say because they fear being called a racist. Yes 33   No   5

34. At the end of Obama's eight years as president, will he be a success or failure? Suc 5   Fail 35

35. Would you have voted for or against the gun law that Congress voted down on April 17, 2013? (Background checks) For 14   Agn   22

36. The US government sent a delegation to Hugo Chavez's funeral in Venezuela but not to Margaret Thatcher's funeral in England. Was this a good decision? Yes 1   No   37

37. Which of these describes your opinion of Obama best? Like 4   Dislike 7   Loathe 20

38. Who was/is the better US president? Geo. W. Bush 32   Obama 4

39. Do you believe that the Obama administration has been honest, fair, and open about the following:

    (a) The Benghazi terrorist attack (ambassador killed) Yes 1   No   38

(b) The Internal Revenue   Yes   2   No   37
    Service (delaying
    tax-exempt status for
    conservative groups

(c) News media (track-   Yes   2   No   37
    ing AP phone calls)

40. Obama made a policy   Yes   2   No   37
    that no US service-
    man can speak at any
    faith-based public
    event. Is that okay?

Funny Questions

1. Do you still drive a car day and night?   Yes 32   No 14
2. Do you exercise often?   Yes 24   No 22
3. Do you still weigh the same as you did when discharged from military?   Yes 16   No 24
4. Do you routinely take prescription drugs most every day?   Yes 14   No 12
   (Viagra doesn't count—that's voluntary.)

About the Author

Robby Campbell was born in 1926 in Mount Vernon, Franklin County, Texas. His birth certificate and discharge papers were in the county clerk's office. He served in WWII in the US Navy. He was in Okinawa when the war ended. His three brothers also served in WWII. Two were in the army, and one was in the air force. He held a bachelor of science degree from the University of Houston and a master of education degree from Texas A&M University in Commerce, Texas (formerly East Texas State College). For additional information about Robby, you can see an interview he did on www.generationsbroadcastceneter.com.

CPSIA information can be obtained
at www.ICGtesting.com
Printed in the USA
LVHW09s0328200818
587422LV00001B/19/P

9 781643 503820